BELIEVING CHRIST

BELIEVING CHRIST

*The Parable of the Bicycle
and Other Good News*

Stephen E. Robinson

Deseret Book Company
Salt Lake City, Utah

DESERET BOOK is a registered trademark of Deseret Book Company.

Visit us at DeseretBook.com

First printing in hardbound 1992
First printing in mass market paperbound 2002

Library of Congress Cataloging-in-Publication Data

Robinson, Stephen Edward
    Believing Christ: the parable of the bicycle and other good news / Stephen E. Robinson
        pages cm
    Includes index.
    ISBN 978-0-87579-634-5 (hardbound)
    ISBN 978-1-57008-926-8 (mass market paperbound)
    1. Salvation. 2. Salvation—Biblical teaching. 3. Grace (Theology) 4. Grace (Theology)—
Biblical teaching. 5. Mormon Church—Doctrines. 6. The Church of Jesus Christ of Latter-
day Saints—Doctrines. I. Title.
BX8643.S25R63   1992
234—dc20   92-20924

Printed in the United States of America
LSC Communications, Harrisonburg, VA

48 47 46 45 44 43 42 41

For Sarah, Rebekah,
Emily, Michael,
Mary, and Leah.
Thanks.

CONTENTS

PREFACE

Since coming to Brigham Young University a few years ago, I have noticed a peculiar and unexpected thing. New freshmen arrive at BYU from wards and branches all over the Church. The majority have been in the Church for a relatively long time, even, I suspect, most of their lives, and they are generally well trained in the peripherals of the gospel. They know a surprising amount about tithing, the Word of Wisdom, genealogy, LDS dating, food storage, and so forth. Of course all of these are important principles for the Latter-day Saints and make up part of the fullness of the gospel in the latter days. But these are not the central doctrines of the gospel as taught in all dispensations from the beginning of the world to its end.

What I noticed about my students was that, as we moved in class from peripheral doctrines and practices of the Church to the central doctrines of the gospel, many of them became less and less sure of themselves — they were soft in the middle. Some were even more comfortable defining themselves in terms of what they *didn't* believe (predestination, original sin, and so forth) than in terms of what they *did* believe. A significant minority did not understand scriptural doctrines such as salvation by grace, justification through faith in Christ, sanctification, atonement, and the meaning and terms of the gospel covenant. They were well taught in the peripherals but not in the vitals of the restored gospel.

I am sure most of this is a function of age and maturity rather than of intelligence and training. Nevertheless, as a result of this discovery, I decided to write several lectures specifically to fill this gap for my students. These lectures were intended to set out the central doctrines, the real "good news" of the gospel, in clear and simple terms drawn both from the scriptures and from practical experience. Since these lectures have met with some success, this book is the logical result.

I thank those who shared with me in the experiences I relate, particularly my wife, Janet, for allowing them to be retold here where they can possibly bless others who may find themselves in similar circumstances. In cases not involving my own family, I have altered some of the names and other descriptive data—but not the experiences—pertaining to individuals. In one case, characteristics of several persons with similar stories have been combined into one character.

I need to say a word here about my wife, Janet, since one of the key experiences related hereafter is mostly hers and is intensely personal, and since someone once suggested that relating it put her in a bad light and made her husband look good at her expense. Janet and I normally think in terms of *us* rather than in terms of *her* or *me*, but if we must compare individual statures, I think the following sketch represents the approximately correct proportions.

When Janet approaches the pearly gates, the Lord may say to the angels something like this, "Why, look everybody—here comes Janet Robinson! Janet's finally here! Let's all go out to welcome her and bring her in." But as he greets her on the steps, he will probably stop and add, "Janet, what on earth is that sorry thing you're dragging behind you?" To which she will respond, "Oh, that? That's my husband. Can I bring him in too?" Without her I haven't got a chance, and this can be confirmed by anyone who knows us well.

I have long maintained that a book without notes is usually not worth reading, since a lack of documentation indicates that the contents are the author's own opinions unsupported by outside scholarship. In this case, I plead guilty. Documenting oneself or one's own experiences, reflections, and views is very hard. Thus readers will either agree with my opinions or disagree, as they choose. Because the material here is personal, I have tried to use the same style I would in the classroom or in conversation, including the colloquial and elliptical, the ironic and the sarcastic. For this I apologize to Miss Wood, my seventh-grade English teacher, who taught me to know better. I claim no outside authority as proof of any of these private opinions, though

I have dutifully inserted as many notes as I could manage in a book of this nature, which though ostensibly theological is also unabashedly devotional. And I would like the reader to know that *I* believe what is said here.

I must also make it clear that I have written this book as a believing Latter-day Saint writing to an audience of other Latter-day Saints. I make no claim of detached scholarly objectivity. If this were a paper for my professional colleagues in the academic field of religion, the methodology and tone would be considerably different. But there is nothing wrong with being bilingual, and in this book I choose to speak the language of faith.

I am frequently asked how a department chair finds the time to write a book. In this case the answer is outstanding secretarial support. Thanks go to Joell Woodbrey for protecting me from nonessentials.

A small part of this book was delivered in May 1990 as a BYU Devotional Address titled "Believing Christ: A Practical Approach to the Atonement," and it appeared both in the November 1990 issue of *BYU Today* and in *Brigham Young University 1989–90 Devotional and Fireside Speeches* (Provo: University Publications, 1990). A slightly revised version of that address was also reprinted in both the *Ensign* and the International Magazines of the Church in April 1992.

Neither this book nor its author has any authority to speak for The Church of Jesus Christ of Latter-day Saints. The ideas expressed here represent a sincerely held but strictly personal point of view.

Chapter One

THE GREAT DILEMMA

For human beings the greatest problem in all the universe, the greatest contradiction, dilemma, or dichotomy there is consists of two simple facts. The first of these two facts is clearly stated in Doctrine and Covenants 1:31: "For I the Lord cannot look upon sin with the least degree of allowance."

This seems a harsh scripture, for it clearly states that God cannot tolerate sin or sinfulness in any degree. He can't wink at it, or ignore it, or turn and look the other way. He won't sweep it under the rug or say, "Well, it's just a little sin. It'll be all right." God's standard, the celestial standard, is absolute, and it allows no exceptions. There is no wiggle room.

Many people seem to have the idea that the Judgment will somehow involve weighing or balancing, with their good deeds on one side of the scales and their bad deeds on the other. If their good deeds outweigh their bad, or if their hearts are basically good and outweigh their sins, then they can be admitted into the presence of God. This notion is false.

As Doctrine and Covenants 1:31 and other scriptures illustrate, God cannot, will not, allow moral or ethical imperfection in any degree whatsoever to dwell in his presence. He cannot tolerate sin "with the *least* degree of *allowance*." It is not a question of whether our good deeds outweigh our sins. If there is even one sin on our record, we are finished. The celestial standard is complete innocence, pure and simple, and nothing less than complete innocence will be tolerated in the kingdom of God. Now whatever you do, *don't stop reading here.* Though it can be depressing to realize how strict God's standards are, there is incredibly good news to follow.

The other horn of the dilemma, the other fact that makes this the greatest of all human problems, is simple enough — I sin every day, and so do you. None of us is innocent in the celestial sense. We fail to be perfect on a more or less regular basis. Our actions are inconsistent with the behavior required for being worthy of the divine presence in the kingdom of God. One of the many scriptures illustrating this can be found in Romans 3:23: "For all have sinned, and come short of the glory of God."

In other words, all human beings, even the best among us, have committed sins or have displayed imperfections that are incompatible with the celestial standard and that God cannot tolerate. Here as elsewhere, Paul implies that there are only two categories: For him either you are perfect or you are a sinner in some degree. There is no middle ground. After all, one little sin was sufficient to get Adam and Eve kicked out of the Garden and out of God's presence. While they were totally innocent, they could walk and talk with him – one transgression, and they were gone.

Now from these two facts – God's absolute demand for perfection and our absolute inability to come up with it – one conclusion is inescapable: *we* cannot be allowed to dwell in the presence of God, sinful and imperfect beings as we are. This contradiction between God's demands and our inability to carry them out represents the most serious problem with the direst consequences in all the universe.

Sometimes we assume that everyone else is doing better than we are. We think that other people are not sinners, that they keep all the commandments all of the time, and we loathe ourselves because we cannot do the same thing. As a result, many of us, often the best among us, despair at what we see as an unbridgeable gap between what God demands and what we do. Thus even the great fisherman, Peter the Rock, said when first confronted by the Master's power, "Depart from me; for I am a sinful man, O Lord." (Luke 5:8.)

Once he saw the power of Jesus Christ and knew that He was genuinely sent from God, Peter could come to only one conclusion – "I'm not worthy. You shouldn't be here with me. If you knew how rotten I am, you'd realize it's hopeless. I'm not like you – I'm sinful. So don't waste your time here on me; go find someone righteous and religious, someone who can be saved. One as holy as you deserves a much better disciple than a poor wretch like me." No one knew better than Peter the vast chasm between the demands of God and the ability of unaided humans to meet those demands. And before he learned the good news, even the great fisherman apparently could see no hope, no way out of the Great Dilemma.

Perhaps I can further illustrate our situation with an analogy taken from my own family experience. I have five lovely daughters, but only one son. I'm pretty hard on Michael, my son, because I love him and because I want him to grow up better than his father did. One day when Michael was five or six years old, he did something that I thought was particularly vile, so I swatted him, yelled at him, and sent him to his room, saying, "And don't you dare come out of your room until I come and get you!"

Then I forgot all about him. Hours passed. I remember that I washed the cars and mowed the lawn, and I was about halfway through a football game on TV when I heard Michael's door open down the long hallway off the living room. "Oh no," I said in self-reproach as I remembered Michael. Leaping to my feet, I ran to the hallway. There at the other end of the hall was my little son. His eyes were swollen, his face was red, and tears were on his cheeks. He was a little nervous and hesitant, for he had been told to stay in his room until I came to get him, but he looked up at me from the other end of the hall and said, "Daddy, isn't there any way we can ever be friends again?"

Well, he broke my heart. I ran to him and hugged him and assured him that no little boy had ever been loved by a father more than he was loved by me.

Spiritually, we are all in the same boat that Michael was in. We all know what it feels like to be "sent to our rooms" spiritually, that is, to be alienated from our Heavenly Father, to be cut off and alone. We experience the pain of the Great Dilemma here in mortality. And knowing better than anyone else our own dreadful inadequacy, sometimes like Peter all we can think to do is to wave the Lord on to someone else more worthy than our sinful selves. This is not a gesture of denial or a rejection of the Savior; rather, it is an expression of our hopelessness.

We have all done things that shame us, and we have felt the horrid weight of guilt and remorse and self-reproach. There are sins that maim us spiritually; sins that may not kill us outright but will fester and will not heal; sins that make us feel as though we've drunk raw sewage or contracted some loathsome disease, as if we can wash but can never get clean. In the grip of such sins and in the midst of guilt and despair, in our terrible aloneness, cut off from God, we raise our eyes to heaven and cry out, "Oh, Father, isn't there any way we can ever be friends again?"

Chapter Two

GOOD NEWS

The answer of all the prophets and all the scriptures to the question of the Great Dilemma is a resounding "YES! Imperfect people can be reconciled to a perfect God and be allowed to dwell in his presence." And even as he answers our question, and by the very means with which he answers it, God assures us that no son or daughter has ever been loved by a mortal father more than we are loved by him. In fact the solution to the Great Dilemma, to the alienation of imperfect humans from their perfect God, is precisely what all the scriptures bear witness of in one way or another. And that solution is called the atonement of Jesus Christ.

Atonement means taking two things that have become separated, estranged, or incompatible, like a perfect God and an imperfect me or you, and bringing them together again, thus making the two be "at one." The word itself derives historically from two smaller words and a suffix *at•one•ment* (to make at one), and the Greek word for *atone* is often translated "to reconcile." Thus, to the two harsh realities mentioned above and recorded in Doctrine and Covenants 1:31 and Romans 3:23, Jesus Christ adds a third reality—the Atonement, the reconciliation, the "good news" of the gospel[1]—that though separated from God, there is a way we can become one with him again.

I am particularly fond of the way the Lord says this in Isaiah 1:18: "Come now, and let us reason together, saith the Lord: though your sins be as scarlet, they shall be as white as snow; though they be red like crimson, they shall be as wool." I would like to expand upon this scripture just a little bit to make sure that the significance of it doesn't get past us. What the Lord is saying here is this: "It doesn't matter what you did. Whatever it was, no matter how horrible or vile, is not the issue. The issue here is that whatever your sin was or is, I can erase it, I can clean you up and make you innocent, pure, and worthy, and I can do it today; I can do it *now*."

BELIEVING CHRIST

Unfortunately, there are many members of the Church who simply do not believe this. Though they claim to have testimonies of Christ and of his gospel, they reject the witness of the scriptures and of the prophets about the good news of Christ's atonement. Often these people naïvely hold on to mutually contradictory propositions without even re-

---

[1]In fact, the Greek word translated in the New Testament as "Gospel" (*euangelion*) means literally "good news."

alizing the nature of the contradiction. For example, they may believe that the Church is true, that Jesus is the Christ, and that Joseph Smith was a prophet of God, while at the same time refusing to accept the possibility of their own complete forgiveness and eventual exaltation in the kingdom of God. They believe *in* Christ, but they do not *believe* Christ. He says, "Though your sins be as scarlet, they shall be as white as snow. I can make you pure and worthy and celestial," and they answer back, "No, you can't. The gospel only works for other people; it won't work for me."

Yet the "good news" of the gospel is good news to me not because it promises that other people who are better than I am can be saved, but because it promises that *I* can be saved—wretched, inadequate, and imperfect me. And until I accept that possibility, until I believe Christ when he says he can bring me into his kingdom and set me on a throne, I have not really accepted the good news of the gospel—I have only accepted the messenger while rejecting his wonderful message.

Faith is the first principle of the gospel, but this does not mean just believing the historical claims of the gospel. Do you believe that the Church is true, that Joseph Smith was a prophet, and that the gospel has been restored in the latter days? Good, but that's not enough. The first Article of Faith specifies that we must have faith in the Lord Jesus Christ. We often think that having faith in Christ means believing in his identity as the Son of God and the Savior of the world. But believing in Jesus' *identity* as the Christ is only the first half of it. The other half is believing in his *ability*, in his *power* to cleanse and to save—to make unworthy sons and daughters worthy.

Not only must we believe that he is who he says he is, we must also believe that he can do what he says he can do. We must not only believe *in* Christ, we must also *believe Christ* when he says he can clean us up and make us celestial. He says that through his atoning blood, all mankind may be saved (see A of F 3)—and "all mankind" must logically include you and me. So until we accept the real possibility of our own exaltation in the kingdom of God, we do not yet have faith in Christ; we do not yet believe.

As a former bishop and as a counselor and teacher in the Church, I have heard many variations on the same theme of doubt. One individual might say, "Oh, bishop, I can't expect the same blessings as the faithful Saints. I can't expect to be exalted in the kingdom of God because I sinned horribly. You see, I did this, or I did that. Of course I'll come to Church and hope for the best, but I can't possibly be exalted after what I did."

Another might say, "You don't understand. I punched my ticket wrong. When I was young, I made choices that took me down a different path, and now, after all those years, I just can't get there from here." Someone else once said, "Oh no, I don't expect to be exalted. I'm nobody. I'm just an *average* member, just an attender. I've always had little jobs in the Church. I've never been a leader, and I don't have any talents. I'll certainly never be the bishop [or the Relief Society president]. I just don't have very much to contribute, so I don't expect to receive very much in the resurrection. I just hope I make the bottom level of the celestial kingdom, but I know I won't be exalted."

My favorite example of this kind of thinking was a man who once said to me, "Look, bishop, I'm just not celestial material." I guess I finally lost my patience and responded by saying, "So what's your point? Of course you're not celestial material. Neither am I, neither is any of us. That's why we need the atonement of Christ, which can *make* us celestial. John, why don't you just admit your real problem — that you don't have any faith in Christ?" Well, he got a little angry at that, for he had been a Protestant before he became a Latter-day Saint, and both as a Protestant and as a Latter-day Saint, he had believed in Jesus Christ. He shot back with, "How dare you say that to me? I know that Jesus is the Christ, the Son of God." "Yes," I replied, "you believe *in* Christ; you just don't believe Christ. He says he can *make* you celestial material, and you have the audacity to sit there and say, 'No, he can't.' You believe all right — you believe Christ makes promises he can't keep."

Each of these four cases represents a variation on the same dismal theme. All of them boil down to this: "I do not believe Christ can do what he claims. I have no faith in his ability to exalt me." If you were to ask these people what their spiritual problems were, they would insist on X, Y, or Z — some unique or special problem encountered down the road some distance on their spiritual journey. But their actual problem is not X, Y, or Z, nor is it unique, nor is it down the road any distance at all. Their real problem is with A number 1 — the very first step. For all four of these objections and many other versions that could have been cited are simply ways of camouflaging the same basic problem—lack of faith in the Lord Jesus Christ.

These people simply won't believe that the gospel can work for them. And without obeying the first principle of the gospel, without having genuine faith in Christ, these individuals cannot enjoy the power and the blessings either of faith in Christ or of the principles that follow faith—repentance, baptism, and the gift of the Holy Ghost. Even though they may consider themselves experienced and mature members of the Church, they have not yet been spiritually born.

If we believe only *in* Christ without believing Christ, then we are like people sitting in cold, dark houses surrounded by unused lamps and heaters, people who believe in electricity but who never throw the switch to turn on the power. People like this often pretend to themselves and to others that merely *believing* in electricity makes them warm and gives them light, but they still shiver in the dark unless they turn on the power. Though the appliances may all work and the wiring may be in good order, until we accept the power itself, beyond merely believing in the theory of power, we cannot enjoy the warmth and the light. This is why genuine faith in Christ—active acceptance of his power and not just passive belief in his identity—is and must be the very first principle of the gospel. No matter how much of the gospel one learns or even believes as a theory, until we accept the reality of our own salvation, we have not yet turned on the power.

THE DEMAND FOR PERFECTION

Often the reason some people can't fully accept the blessings of the gospel is because the weight of the demand for perfection has driven them to despair. They mistakenly feel that in order for the Atonement to work in their lives, they must first become perfect through their own efforts. But anyone who could meet this requirement would not need the Atonement at all, for such a person would already be reconciled to God, having achieved the celestial standard of perfection on his or her own without needing Christ and his atonement – and this is not possible.

Let me emphasize again, the good news is not that perfect people can be reconciled to God, but that *imperfect* people can be. Whenever I hear someone say that they are going to perfect themselves, I cringe. I want to ask, "Do you really think that exaltation is a matter of reaching down into your guts and pulling out the energy and determination you need to live a perfect life? If so, you don't want a savior, you want to do it all yourself."

Now it is true that in order to receive a celestial glory, we must become perfect. And we are quite conscientious about telling each other how perfect we must be. In fact, sometimes no matter how well we do in any area of our lives, some well-intentioned Saint seems to be right there to point out that we aren't perfect and that we must do better next time. Many of us tell ourselves this same thing time after time, no matter how well we may actually do, and never allow ourselves even the smallest taste of deserved personal satisfaction.

THE SHORTCUT TO PERFECTION

Yes, we are very good at telling each other and ourselves how perfect we must be to inherit the kingdom. It's just that too often we forget to tell each other how this perfection is to be gained. You see, there is a trick to it—a shortcut. And if you don't know the trick, the shortcut to perfection, you can burn yourself out trying to become perfect on your own.[2] The great secret is this: Jesus Christ will share *his* perfection, *his* sinlessness, *his* righteousness, *his* merits with us. In his mercy he offers us the use of his perfection, in the absence of our own, to satisfy the demands of justice.

In the short run we are considered perfect, accepted as perfect, by becoming one with a perfect Christ. In the long run, this makes it possible for us actually to become perfect in our own right at some future time, but that time is long after the Judgment and long after we have already inherited the kingdom of God through the merit, mercy, and perfection of Jesus Christ. Thus the most important goal in mortality is becoming one with Christ through the gospel covenant and gaining access through that union to his perfection, rather than remaining separate and aloof while trying (fruitlessly!) to generate our own perfection and thereby save ourselves.

Let me illustrate. A number of years ago our family lived in Williamsport, Pennsylvania. Things were pretty good there. We owned our own little home in a nice neighborhood,

---

[2]Here as elsewhere, I have used a figure of speech for effect. In truth, there is no shortcut, or "long cut" for that matter. Christ is the *only* way.

and we liked our neighbors. I had a good job at a local college and was doing well in my career. Our family seemed happy enough. We had family home evening and family prayers regularly, and Janet and I said our prayers together every night. We held temple recommends and attended the temple as often as possible. I was in the bishopric in the local ward, and Janet was the Relief Society president.

Janet had a particularly exciting year that year. Besides being Relief Society president, she graduated from college for the second time (in accounting), she passed the CPA exam and took a job with a local firm, and she gave birth to our fourth child (Michael)—all in her spare time, of course. Actually, Janet was under a lot of pressure that year, but like many husbands, I didn't notice or appreciate how much pressure she was under until something blew. And blow it did.

One day the lights just went out. It was as though Janet had died to spiritual things; she had burned out. She became very passive in her attitude toward the Church. When her Relief Society counselors called her, she told them that they could do whatever they wanted to, that she had asked to be released from her calling. One of the worst aspects of this sudden change was that Janet wouldn't talk about it; she wouldn't tell me what was wrong.

Finally, after almost two weeks, I made her mad with my nagging one night as we lay in bed, and she said, "All right. Do you want to know what's wrong? I'll tell you what's wrong—I can't do it anymore. I can't lift it. My load is just too heavy. I can't do all the things I'm supposed to.

I can't get up at 5:30, and bake bread, and sew clothes, and help the kids with their homework, and do my own homework, and make their lunches, and do the housework, and do my Relief Society stuff, and have scripture study, and do my genealogy, and write my congressman, and go to PTA meetings, and get our year's supply organized, and go to my stake meetings, and write the missionaries . . . " She just started naming, one after the other, all the things she couldn't do or couldn't do perfectly—all the individual bricks that had been laid on her back in the name of perfection until they had crushed the light out of her.

"I try not to yell at the kids," she continued, "but I can't seem to help it; I get mad, and I yell. So then I try not to get mad, but I eventually do. I try not to have hard feelings toward this person and that person, but I do. I'm just not very Christlike. No matter how hard I try to love everyone, I fail. I don't have the talent Sister X has, and I'm just not as sweet as Sister Y. Steve, I'm just not perfect—I'm never going to be perfect, and I just can't pretend anymore that I am. I've finally admitted to myself that I can't make it to the celestial kingdom, so why should I break my back trying?"

Well, that was the beginning of one of the longest nights of our life together. I asked Janet, "Do you have a testimony?" She responded, "Of course I do—that's what's so terrible. I know the gospel is true, I just can't live up to it." I asked her if she had kept her baptismal covenants, and she replied, "No. I've tried and I've tried, but I can't keep all the commandments all the time." I asked her if she had kept the covenants she had made in the temple, and again she said, "I try, but no matter how hard I try, I don't seem to be able to do all that's asked of me."

Now I need to make it clear at this point that the reason I proposed marriage to Janet many years ago was because she is the finest, sweetest, most genuinely loving and selfless person I have ever met. So what she was telling me just didn't add up. So we went back and forth for some time with her cataloging all her faults, inadequacies, and imperfections, and with me knowing she was a better person than most and trying to find out what was really wrong. Finally it occurred to me what the problem was, and frankly, I was astounded. Here I was supposed to be a "doctor" in the field of religion, and I couldn't see Mt. Everest right in front of my nose. What I realized finally was that Janet did not completely understand the core of the gospel — the atonement of Christ. She knew the demands, but not the good news.

Who would have thought that after all the meetings and lessons, after all the talks and testimonies and family home evenings, somehow the heart of the gospel had escaped her? She knew and believed everything except the most important part. You see, Janet was trying to save herself. She was trying to do it all with Jesus Christ as merely an advisor. Janet knew why Jesus can be called a coach, a cheerleader, an advisor, a teacher, the elder brother, the head of the Church, and even God. She understood all of that, but she didn't understand why he is called the *Savior*.

BEING SAVED

But do Latter-day Saints believe in "being saved"? If I ask my classes on campus that question with just the right Southern drawl in my voice, I can usually get about a third of them to shake their heads and say, "No. We don't believe in 'being saved.' That's those other guys, the ones on TV." What a tragedy! Of course the Latter-day Saints believe in being saved. They do now, and they always have. How can Jesus be called the Savior if he never saves anybody?

That's like having a lifeguard who won't get out of his chair or who won't get wet — "Well, look at that. There's another one going under out there. Gee, that's too bad!" Such a lifeguard may even shout out helpful advice like, "Try the backstroke!" But if he won't get wet, what good is he? And what good is a Savior who doesn't save anybody? It is the whole message of the Book of Mormon, as it is of the Bible, that Jesus Christ is the Savior of the world. Yes, the Latter-day Saints believe in being saved. But Janet, like so many others, was trying to save herself, and she couldn't do it. In fact, no one can, not even the best among us.

The Brother of Jared. For example, look at Ether 3:2 in the Book of Mormon. The speaker is the brother of Jared, one of the greatest prophets who ever lived. His faith was so great that, as is recorded in this chapter, he was able to pierce the veil and see God. But look at how this good and faithful man approached God. "Now behold, O Lord, and do not be angry with thy servant because of his weakness before thee; for we know that thou art holy and dwellest in the heavens, and that we are unworthy before thee." Imagine that! Here was one of the great prophets of all time, and he began his prayer with an apology for his weakness and his unworthiness. Certainly he was under no illusions about being perfect.

He went on to say, "Because of the fall our natures have become evil continually." All this means is that as a result of the Fall of Adam, human beings are subject to the natural conditions of mortality. As long as we are in the flesh, we will have to wrestle with the flesh, with our carnal natures, and occasionally the flesh will win. Such a defeat is always wrong, and we will be held accountable, but it is *going* to happen from time to time.

We can expect this struggle to go on as long as we live. Each of us has experienced this opposition of the carnal self in one way or another. For example, from time to time I will tell my carnal self, "Flesh, today we are going to diet!" To which my flesh inevitably responds with something like, "In your dreams, Bozo," and then sets up the steady chant, "Hot fudge! Hot fudge! Hot fudge!" This opposition of the flesh, the carnal self, is not something that we can overcome once and for all while in mortality. As long as we are in mortality, our carnal nature will be prone to evil continually, to paraphrase the brother of Jared.

My personal belief is that in the resurrection the opposition of the flesh will finally be overcome. In mortality, the spirit and the body are two separate entities forced to coexist in the same person. The mortal connection between them is both recent and temporary, hence they wrestle and fidget with each other. But in the resurrection, body and spirit become one thing. They will be inseparably united, welded together, and will speak with one voice – the voice of the unified self, of the soul in the strict sense. (See D&C 88:15.) But until then, we must wrestle with ˄ separate, carnal self. And from time to time, even the best among us, like the brother of Jared, will lose a struggle.

But this is not the most important part of what the brother of Jared has to say in Ether 3:2. The most important part comes at the end of the verse: "Nevertheless, O Lord, thou hast given us a commandment that we must call upon thee, that from thee we may receive according to our desires." It doesn't really matter in the long run that the brother of Jared is unworthy from the celestial point of view. In that respect he is no different from all other human beings. The point is that God has commanded us, unworthy though we may be, to call upon him anyway, because he has prepared a way for us to receive what we desire *despite* our imperfection. Notice that he says, "according to our desires" and not strictly "according to our merits" or "according to our works," or according to any other combination some of us might expect. (See D&C 137:9.)

What matters is that through the atonement of Jesus Christ we can receive, despite our unworthiness, what we desire, what we long for – but only if it *is* what we really long for. So what do you want? What do you *really* want? In Matthew 5:6 the Lord says: "Blessed are they which do hunger and thirst after righteousness: for they shall be filled." We regularly misinterpret this scripture to mean something like "Blessed are the righteous." But that is not what it means at all. When are we hungry? When do we thirst? *After* Thanksgiving dinner with all the trimmings? No, we are hungry when we haven't eaten; we are thirsty when we haven't drunk, when we don't have the object of our desire.

This beatitude refers to people like you and me who want to do what is right, who long for, who hunger and thirst after righteousness — the pure righteousness of God, the perfect righteousness and absolute innocence of the celestial kingdom. Blessed are they who desire with all their hearts to be righteous as Christ is righteous, to be perfect as he is perfect, who long for it and seek it, and who would give anything for it, though they do not have it. What is their reward? They shall, through the atonement of Christ, receive it according to their fondest desires! In the words of the beatitude, "they shall be filled."

The Example of Nephi. Let's take a look at another prophetic example from the Book of Mormon. In 2 Nephi 4:17–19, Nephi wrote: "O wretched man that I am! Yea, my heart sorroweth because of my flesh; my soul grieveth because of mine iniquities. I am encompassed about, because of the temptations and the sins which do so easily beset me. And when I desire to rejoice, my heart groaneth because of my sins." Wait a minute. Iniquities? Temptations? Sins? There must be some mistake here. This scripture must be Laman or Lemuel talking, the wicked sons; surely this can't be Nephi. Nephi was the *righteous* son.

No, of course there is no mistake. This *is* Nephi, another

of the greatest prophets who ever lived. And this isn't even the teenaged Nephi. The scripture comes from 2 Nephi, when the family was already in the New World. This is the mature Nephi speaking, the Nephi of experience and wisdom, allowing us to see into his very heart. And Nephi, like the brother of Jared, or like the Apostle Paul (see 1 Tim. 1:15), was under no illusions about his own perfection. Nephi knew and regretted that he sometimes lost his battle with the flesh, that he was easily tempted, that he sinned.

But once again, the fact that Nephi was imperfect, that he failed to qualify on the basis of his own efforts and merits for the kingdom of God, that he just plain messed up sometimes, is not the point. Every human being, with the exception of Jesus Christ alone, has failed to keep all the commandments all the time. We may fail by differing degrees, but we all fail. That is why we all need help, why we all need a Savior, and why needing help and needing a Savior are no disgrace. This is the real focus, the real point, of what Nephi said here, "Nevertheless, I know in whom I have trusted. . . . He hath filled me with his love, even unto the consuming of my flesh." (2 Ne. 4:19, 21.)

Even though Nephi was discouraged and depressed by his inability to live perfectly, he trusted the Savior to get him to the kingdom anyway. He *trusted* the Savior and was confident in the Savior's love. Then to combine all three verses and paraphrase, Nephi was saying, "No, I'm not perfect. Yes, my faults bother me, and yes, I wish I did a better job. Nevertheless, I have faith in Jesus Christ, I trust him. He says he can get me into his kingdom despite my imperfections, and I believe him. I know he loves me, and I trust him to continue saving me from all my enemies."

Unfortunately, unlike Nephi, many of us just don't trust the Savior. We believe in him, but we don't *trust* him. We get so frightened and intimidated, so horrified, by our own imperfections that we don't see how he can possibly save us from them, and we lose faith. But if these great prophets had a healthy sense of their own sins and shortcomings, and yet could still confidently maintain that they had a place in the kingdom of God, should we not learn from their examples of trust and confidence — their examples of faith?

Besides fear of one's own imperfection, there are other reasons why some people cannot trust the Savior. Many people fear that if they commit themselves to him and try to live the gospel loyally and faithfully, they will miss something important that the world has to offer. Often they fear that a total commitment to Christ and the Church would mean being exploited or being left unfulfilled emotionally, intellectually, or physically. There are those who want the Church in their lives but are afraid of a full embrace. The bottom line for all such is the same — even though they may believe in him, they do not trust him. They do not yet have genuine faith in Christ.

HOW PERFECTION COMES

Part of the good news of the gospel is the knowledge that finally perfection comes, to those who desire it, through the atonement of Christ instead of solely through their own efforts. When we become one with Christ in the gospel

23

covenant, we gain access to *his* perfection. It's as though two people with separate bank accounts got married and formed a joint account. When Janet and I got married, my checking account was overdrawn, but Janet had money in hers. After the wedding, we went to the bank and merged our accounts to create a single, joint account. As far as the bank was concerned, I was no longer just Stephen Robinson, and she was no longer just Janet Bowen. Now we were Stephen and Janet Robinson. A new partnership had been created that included the assets and liabilities of both its component parts. And since Janet had more assets than I had liabilities, the new account had a positive balance. It was like a miracle! Just by entering into a marriage covenant and becoming one with Janet, I was on firm financial ground for the first time in months.

This makes an excellent analogy for what happens when we enter into the gospel covenant. The Savior, who has infinite assets, proposes a merger with the individual, who has finite liabilities. I use the word "proposes" by design, for the relationship proposed is often referred to in scripture as a marriage, and it is certainly as intimate and bonding as a marriage. This is why Christ is often called the Bridegroom (e.g., Matt. 25:1–13; John 3:29) and why the Church (or Israel) is often referred to as the Bride (e.g., Hosea 2:19; Rev. 21:2, D&C 109:74).

As husband and wife become one with each other through the covenant of marriage, so the Savior and the saved become one with each other through the covenant of the gospel. (Cf. 1 Cor. 6:15–17.) Just as a bride renounces all competing claims upon her loyalties and normally takes her husband's last name, so those who enter this covenant with Christ renounce all competing loyalties, put him first, and take his name upon them. To this union, we bring our righteous desires and our loyalty. He brings his perfection. In the covenant union, what is mine becomes his, and what is his becomes mine. Thus my sins become his for payment, and his righteousness becomes mine for justification.

When we become one with Jesus Christ, spiritually we form a partnership with a joint account, and his assets and our liabilities flow into each other. Since he has more assets than we have liabilities (he has an infinite ocean of assets), the new account has a positive balance as soon as it is formed, and the partnership is justified, even though its junior partners (you and me) could not make it on their own. This is what the Apostle Paul refers to as being "in Christ" (1 Cor. 1:1) and what Moroni calls being "perfect in Christ" (Moro. 10:32).

Taken together, Christ and I make up a new creature. The old creature, the imperfect me, ceases to exist, and a glorious new creature, a perfect partnership, takes its place. Taken together as a single entity, the two of us, Christ and I, are perfect. I do *not* mean (this is absolutely crucial!) that we can *become* perfect later on. I mean that from the moment the partnership is formed in good faith, from the moment we have sincere faith in Christ, sincerely repent of our sins, and receive baptism and the gift of the Holy Ghost—from this moment the partnership is celestial. The merits of the Senior Partner make it so. True, this is not *individual* perfection, which will indeed come later (much later), rather it is perfection-in-Christ (see Moro. 10:32–33), through which we receive the benefits of our partner's merits. Nevertheless, from this moment the kingdom is ours, provided that we maintain the partnership by abiding in the gospel covenant. (See 3 Ne. 27:16, 19–21.)

At this point someone will object that I still have faults and limitations, and I admit that if I am judged separately and alone, this is true. But in the covenant relationship, I am not judged separately and alone but as one with Christ. Simply consider the mathematics of it: If Christ is infinite and unlimited, but I am finite and limited, and we become one, what do Christ and I together add up to? What is the sum of an infinite, positive quantity and a limited, negative quantity ($\infty + -x$)? Why, infinity, of course! And the math is the same whether I (the finite part) am a ten or a five or a one, whether I'm the prophet or a stake president or any other struggling member. Infinity plus *any* amount, positive or negative, equals infinity.

What matters is not how much we bring to the equation, but only that we can *make* the equation by entering into a covenant relationship with an infinite Christ, however great or small we may think ourselves to be. Any two people who are joined together and have become one in a covenant unity are perfect as long as one of them is Jesus Christ.

In Doctrine and Covenants 76:68–69, Joseph Smith described the inhabitants of the celestial kingdom in these terms: "These are they whose names are written in heaven, where God and Christ are the judge of all. These are they who are just men *made perfect through Jesus* the mediator of the new covenant, who wrought out this perfect atonement through the shedding of his own blood." (Italics added.) Those who inherit the celestial kingdom are *just* men and women, that is, men and women who want justice, who hunger and thirst after righteousness.[3] They are good neighbors, and they do the best they can. This makes them just—good people. These good people are then *made* perfect through the perfect atonement of a perfect Christ.

You see, you can make yourself *just* in one sense of the word. Your own efforts will suffice to make you a good person, even a righteous person in relative human terms. One certainly doesn't need the gospel to be a good person in terms of personal life-style (indeed, one can even be hostile to the gospel and still be comparatively good). You can, by your own efforts, become an honorable person and thereby qualify on your own merits for an approximately terrestrial glory. (Cf. D&C 76:75.)

But you can't make yourself perfect. You can't make yourself sinless and worthy of the presence of God the Father. You can't make yourself celestial, no matter how hard you try, because you have already sinned, and sinlessness requires not only perfect performance in the future, but also perfect performance in the past. Otherwise, you are not

---

[3]The words *just* and *righteous* are the same both in Greek and in Hebrew. They are used in the scriptures two different ways to mean (a) *perfectly* just or righteous in the celestial sense (e.g., Acts 7:52 or Rom. 3:10) or (b) *relatively* just or righteous compared with the rest of the world (e.g., Matt. 5:45). Here the sense is the latter.

sinless, you are just a sinner who hasn't sinned *recently*. Many an obsessive student has learned the sad truth that once he or she gets just one *B*, no number of *A*'s thereafter will restore a perfect record, a 4.0 grade-point average. Innocence requires forgiveness and cleansing. It requires that the record be expunged and rewritten, that all the sinful former deeds and actions cease to be counted — and all these things come only through the atonement of Christ. You can make yourself *just* and terrestrial by your own good works and best efforts, but only Christ can make you *perfect* and celestial.

The Corporate Analogy. Some of my students who are business majors prefer the following analogy. If two companies, one totally bankrupt and the other incredibly profitable, should merge to create a single, new corporation, what happens to the debts of the weaker company? They are paid out of the profits of the stronger, and the corporation, the combination of the two, is judged to be financially sound. As long as there is more being produced by the one than is being lost through the other, the corporation is in the black. It is profitable. It is financially justified.

The same is true in the spiritual parallel. When we enter into the covenant of the gospel and become one with Christ, we create a new corporate entity, a partnership, that is *immediately* profitable and *immediately* justified through the infinite merits of the Savior (the only really profitable enterprise). And as long as we don't dissolve the partnership, we are justified by his merits in that unique relationship. As an individual, I may have no hope, but as a junior partner in a joint venture with Christ, I have every assurance of success.

The Athletic Analogy. Some of my students are more comfortable with examples or illustrations taken from athletics than from business or finance, so I sometimes like to compare the covenant relationship to team sports. In team sports, it doesn't matter which of the players makes the points. When one individual scores, the whole team scores. If the quarterback throws a touchdown ball to the tight end, then it doesn't matter that the guards never touched the ball, or even that the defense was sitting on the bench. It doesn't matter that some on the team may have missed their blocks or run the wrong routes. It doesn't even matter that the second or third string hadn't yet been in the game. When one member of the team scores, the whole team scores. In terms of who wins, it doesn't matter whether we are on the offense or the defense, in the backfield or line, or on the first-string, second-string, or special teams. The entire team wins, not just the individual who makes the winning score.

In making the gospel covenant, we become part of a team whose captain and quarterback is Jesus Christ, a cosmic Heisman Trophy winner who throws nothing but touchdowns. If we are on his team, we will go undefeated. Even if I miss my block now and then, even if he asks me just to sit on the bench most of the time, as long as he's the captain, we're going to win. But I've got to be on *his* team, not my own and not somebody else's.

Alternatively, the gospel covenant could be compared to

29

a long-distance race. Normally, we think of only one winner in a race, but in the gospel race, all who finish win. In addition, the differences in their finishing times are irrelevant. Some people will have good times and some will not, but the only losers are those who give up and quit before they reach the goal. In the gospel race, there are no losers, only quitters. Those who run across the finish line in minutes, those who walk across it in hours, or those who crawl across it in days all win the prize. For they all endured to the end, according to their talents and abilities, looking to the Savior. Paul used this analogy, writing, "Let us run with patience the race that is set before us, looking unto Jesus the author and finisher of our faith." (Heb. 12:1–2.) Too many of us expend our precious energy worrying about our relative times instead of keeping our eyes on the goal, putting one foot in front of the other, and enduring to the end.

THE PARABLE OF THE BICYCLE

As Janet and I discussed these things on that dark night years ago, nothing really seemed to be getting through to her. Then I remembered something that had happened in our family just a few months before and that we now refer to at our house as the parable of the bicycle.

One afternoon after work as I sat reading the newspaper, our oldest daughter, Sarah, who was then seven years old, came up to me and said, "Daddy, can I get a bike? I'm the only kid in our neighborhood who doesn't have a bike." I mumbled some kind of general and nonspecific assent, but

Sarah lifted up the paper and looked me in the eye. "How, and when?" she asked.

Now it would not have been easy for us financially to buy Sarah a bicycle at that particular time, so I tried to stall her. "I'll tell you what, Sarah," I said. "You save all your pennies, and pretty soon you'll have enough for a bike."

"OK," she said, and she went away—I was off the hook. A few weeks went by, and I was once again sitting in my chair after work, reading the newspaper. This time I was aware of Sarah doing some chore for her mother and being paid for it. Then she went into her bedroom, and I heard a sound like "clink, clink."

"Sarah, what are you doing?" I asked. She came out of her bedroom with a little jar in her hand. It had once been a maraschino cherry jar, but she had cleaned it up and cut a slot in the lid. On the bottom of the jar were a bunch of coins. Sarah showed me the jar and said, "You promised that if I saved all my pennies, pretty soon I'd have enough to get a bike. And Daddy, I've saved every single one!"

Well, she's my daughter, and I love her. I hadn't actually lied to her. If she saved all of her pennies, eventually she *would* have enough for a bike. But by then, she would probably want a car. In the meantime, sweet little Sarah was doing everything in her power to follow my instructions, but her needs were still not being met. I was overwhelmed. "OK, Sarah," I said, "let's go downtown and look at bikes."

We went to every store in Williamsport. Finally, in one of the big discount stores, we found it: the Perfect Bicycle (probably the one she knew in the premortal life). From halfway across the store, she knew it was The One. She ran and jumped up on the bike and said, "Dad, this is it. This is just the one I want." She was thrilled.

Then she noticed the price tag hanging down between the handlebars, and with a smile, she reached down and turned it over. At first she just stared at it; then the smile disappeared. Her face clouded up, and she started to cry. "Oh Daddy," she said in despair, "I'll never have enough for a bicycle." It was her first bitter dose of adult reality.

The bike, as I recall, cost over one hundred dollars. It was hopelessly beyond her means. But because Sarah is my daughter and I love her, I have an interest in her happiness. So I asked, "Sarah, how much money *do* you have?"

"Sixty-one cents," she answered forlornly.

"Then I'll tell you what, dear. Let's try a different arrangement. You give me everything you've got, the whole sixty-one cents, and a hug and a kiss, and this bike is yours."

Well, she's never been stupid. She gave me a big hug and a kiss and handed over the sixty-one cents. Then I had to drive home very slowly because she wouldn't get off the bike. She rode it home on the sidewalk (it was only a few blocks), and I drove along beside her. And as I drove, it occurred to me that this was a parable for the atonement of Christ.

You see, we all want something desperately, but it's not a bicycle. We want the kingdom of God. We want to go home to our heavenly parents worthy and clean. But the horrible price — perfect performance — is hopelessly beyond our means. At some point in our spiritual progress, we realize what the full price of admission into that kingdom is, and we also realize that we cannot pay it. And then we despair. That's where Janet was that night as we talked, in despair at the vast difference between perfect performance and what she felt she could do.

But only at this point, when we finally realize our inability to perfect and save ourselves, when we finally realize our truly desperate situation here in mortality and our need to be saved from it by some outside intervention — only then can we fully appreciate the One who comes to save.

At that point, the Savior steps in and says, "So you've done all you can do, but it's not enough. Well, don't despair. I'll tell you what, let's try a different arrangement. How much *do* you have? How much *can* fairly be expected of you? You give me exactly that much (the whole sixty-one cents) and do all you *can* do, and I will provide the rest for now. You give me all you've got and a hug and a kiss (that is, make this a *personal* relationship), and the kingdom is yours! Perfection will still be our ultimate goal, but until you can get it on your own, I'll let you use mine. What do you say? You do everything you *can* do, and I'll do what you can't yet do. Between the two of us, we'll have it all covered. You will be one hundred percent justified."

As Janet and I discussed these things that night, for some reason this particular illustration reached her. When she considered the Atonement and the gospel covenant in this way, she saw how it worked, and a remarkable transformation took place. She just bloomed. I remember her saying through her tears something like this, "I've always had a testimony of the Savior and believed that he is the Son of God. I have always believed that he suffered and died for me. But now I know that he can *save* me, that he can save me from myself, from my sins, from my weakness, from my lack of talent."

Since that time, Janet's experience has helped others both in and out of the Church. Experience has taught us that she is not alone, that there are many who want to serve God and keep his commandments, who hunger and thirst after righteousness, but who, because of the very loftiness and nobility of their desires, despair at the reality of their performance. To all of them we declare, "Christ is the answer. He is the bridge from here to there. He is the solution to the Great Dilemma."

"Ask, and it shall be given you; seek, and ye shall find; knock, and it shall be opened unto you: for every one that asketh receiveth; and he that seeketh findeth; and to him that knocketh it shall be opened." (Matt. 7:7–8.)

This is good news indeed.

Chapter Three

THE COVENANT

A covenant is a contract, an agreement with terms and obligations binding upon both parties. In modern times we validate a contract and make it binding and legal by having both parties sign it. In ancient times covenants were validated and made binding by shedding the blood of a sacrificial animal. Hence, the Hebrew idiom for making a covenant is "to *cut* a covenant." The blood of the sacrificial victim was called "the blood of the covenant," and when it was shed, the terms of the contract were considered to be in force and binding upon both contracting parties.

An example that illustrates this is provided in the Old Testament when God made the covenant of Sinai with his people through Moses. There the contract was finalized by sacrificing oxen, and after the people had agreed to the terms of the covenant, the blood of the covenant sacrifices was sprinkled upon them. (See Ex. 24:3–8.)

By definition, a covenant is a mutual obligation. Therefore it is not possible to have a unilateral covenant, a covenant that involves or binds only one party. A one-sided obligation is simply a debt, or slavery, rather than a covenant relationship. An oath can be one-sided, but a covenant must contain mutual obligation — "if you will do A, I will do B." In the Old Testament period, the covenant between God and his people always had specific terms, and as long as the chosen people kept their part of the contract, God kept his part. However, the reverse was also true, for when the people broke the covenant, God was no longer bound to it either. For example, in 2 Kings 18:12, God did not keep his covenant obligation to save Israel from her enemies because Israel had already broken her contract by disobeying the commandments agreed upon in Exodus 24:3–8. God is bound by his own word to keep the terms of his covenants as long as we keep our part of the bargain. (See D&C 82:10; 84:39–40.)

In the Old Testament the Lord told Israel that there would someday be a *new* covenant — a new relationship between God and his chosen people — superior to that offered through the law of Moses. (See Jer. 31:31–33.) That promise was fulfilled when the covenant of the gospel superseded the covenant of Sinai at the death and resurrection of Jesus Christ. Like the old covenant, this new and everlasting covenant also has a sacrificial victim — Jesus Christ himself, "the Lamb of God" (John 1:29) and "the Lamb that was slain" (Rev. 5:6, 9, 12). The blood of Jesus Christ, shed in Gethsemane and upon the cross, is the blood of the new covenant that, as it was shed, rendered the agreement valid and binding. (See Luke 22:20; 1 Cor. 11:25.)[1]

Just as Moses put the blood of the old covenant upon the chosen people in Exodus 24:8 to signify their acceptance of the contract, so those who accept the new covenant must similarly take the sacrificial blood of Christ upon them. When we take Christ's blood upon us, when we are washed in "the blood of the Lamb" (Rev. 7:14), we are bound to the new covenant in much the same way the children of Israel were bound to the old. When the blood of Christ was shed, the new contract between God and human beings, the gospel covenant, became valid and binding for all those who have agreed to its terms.

JUSTIFICATION

When human beings keep their covenants, when they abide by the conditions of their agreements with God, they are said to be justified. To be justified means to be declared innocent, to be acquitted of all charges of misconduct, to stand guiltless before the law. *Justified* has a strong courtroom or judgment nuance to it and emphasizes the "not guilty" verdict. To be justified, then, is to be declared by God to be not guilty, to be free from any taint of sin and to be acquitted of all our obligations toward him. Thus, being justified is logically equivalent to being declared worthy of the kingdom and presence of God.

---

[1]The Greek word *diathēkē*, which is translated "testament" in these passages, also means "covenant." The New Testament is at the same time the New Covenant.

Justification is a noble aspiration and a necessary condition of exaltation in the kingdom of God. Both the old covenant of the law of Moses and the new covenant of the gospel were designed to justify the individual who entered into and kept his or her covenant. However, the covenant of Moses used the law of justice as its basis for accomplishing this (justification by law), while the gospel covenant uses the law of mercy (justification by faith).

JUSTIFICATION BY LAW

Theoretically, one way of being justified, of receiving a "not guilty" verdict from God, is to keep all the commandments all the time — never to commit a sin and therefore never to be guilty. This is called justification by (keeping) the law or justification by works. Any system that defines righteousness exclusively as a status gained and deserved by personally keeping a specific set of rules is a system of justification by works or by law. In such a system an individual is thought to earn his or her own way into the kingdom of God by not sinning in the first place. This happy solution to the problem of sin eliminates the need for forgiveness, repentance, or atonement. Consequently, however, there is also no need for a savior. The Apostle Paul in his New Testament writings characterized the old covenant of Moses as a system of justification by law or by works.

The terms of the old contract, the law of Moses, were essentially that if the children of Israel "kept the commandments," that is, observed all 613 commands and prohibitions of the law of Moses, God would save them from

38

their enemies and grant them the promised land and a posterity. If both sides kept their part of the bargain, Israel would be God's chosen people, and he would be their God. This covenant was based on strict obedience and on the law of justice.

In practice the rabbis knew that no one keeps all the rules all the time, but they trusted in the mercy of God to somehow atone for mistakes. However, technically there was no scriptural basis for such an expectation. As Deuteronomy 27:26 makes very clear, if you keep the law one hundred percent, you are righteous, but if you break just one of its provisions, you are a sinner, a cursed transgressor of the law. (See also James 2:10.) Still, under the old covenant of the law of Moses, individuals theoretically could by their own efforts and merits make themselves worthy by keeping all the rules all the time.

Technically, there was nothing wrong with the old covenant and its law. It was the word of God. It was just and fair. If the people had just kept their end of the agreement, they would have been justified by the law. After all, anyone who does absolutely everything God commands is, by even the strictest definition, just.

Unfortunately, it turned out that nobody could do it. Just as telling my daughter Sarah to save her pennies for a bicycle may have been plausible in theory but didn't really meet her needs in the real world, so justification by law, though it may be valid in theory, fails in practice to address our real human needs in our actual predicament. Because of our human weaknesses and our fallen natures, the terms of the law of Moses, the old covenant, are simply beyond our ability and therefore don't justify us. Theoretically they could, but in actuality they don't. Justification by obedience to law, or justification by works, is an impossibility because all human beings but one have been *disobedient* at some time or other. And we can't claim to be justified by obedience if we are occasionally *dis*obedient.

As Paul points out, *trying* to keep the commandments is a long way from *actually* keeping them. According to him, anyone stupid enough to trust his own ability to keep all the rules makes the atonement of Christ ineffectual in his own life. (See Gal. 5:4.) Moreover, anyone who wants to trust entirely in his own righteousness needs to be reminded that righteousness through law requires perfect performance: "For as many as are of the works of the law are under the curse: for it is written, Cursed is every one that continueth not *in all things* which are written in the book of the law to do them. But that no man is justified by the law in the sight of God, it is evident: for, The just shall live by faith. And the law is not of faith: but, The man that *doeth* them shall live in them. Christ hath redeemed us from the curse of the law." (Gal. 3:10–13; italics added.)

Paul points out that any claim to righteousness based on one's own efforts to keep the commandments requires a perfect record. One slip and you are no longer perfect, you have become a sinner – and in this sense we are all sinners. "For we have before proved both Jews and Gentiles, that they are all under sin; as it is written, There is none righteous, no, not one. . . . Therefore by the deeds of the law there shall no flesh be justified in his sight: for by the law is the knowledge of sin." (Rom. 3:9–10, 20.)

In other words, since everyone has broken the law, no one can claim to be righteous by virtue of having kept the law. To make matters worse, the law itself pronounces the curse on anyone who is not perfect in keeping all the commandments. (See Deut. 27:26.) Yet because of our fallen natures, it was frankly impossible for human beings to keep all the terms of the old covenant. Therefore, at least from the perspective of Paul in the first century, God in his mercy has provided a new covenant, an agreement with terms we can keep.[2] Jesus Christ is the one who redeems us from the curse of the law—from the demand for perfect performance—by offering a new means of justification, not by law (keeping all the rules all the time), but by faith in Christ. Although it seems that many naïvely attempt justification by works, or self-justification, such an attempt constitutes a false trail. Both the Bible and the Book of Mormon insist that justification cannot be gained in this way:

> Knowing that a man is not justified by the works of the law, but by the faith of [in] Jesus Christ, . . . that we might be justified by the faith of [in] Christ, and not by the works of the law: for by the works of the law shall no flesh be justified. (Gal. 2:16.)

And men are instructed sufficiently that they

---

[2]In actuality this new covenant, what the Lord called "mine everlasting covenant, even the fulness of my gospel" (D&C 66:2), had been offered to many in the past, to Adam, Enoch, Noah, Abraham, and others.

know good from evil. And the law is given unto
men. And by the law no flesh is justified; or, by
the law men are cut off. . . . There is no flesh that
can dwell in the presence of God, save it be
through the merits, and mercy, and grace of the
Holy Messiah. (2 Ne. 2:5–8.)

To summarize then—we can't justify ourselves on our
own. We can't earn our way into the celestial kingdom by
keeping all the commandments. We could in theory, but
we can't in practice—because neither you nor I nor anybody
else has kept *all* the commandments. This is so incredibly
self-evident and simple that some people can't see it. Think
about it. We have already broken some commandment
somewhere, so we cannot claim righteousness on the
grounds that we *keep* the commandments. We are already
disqualified! Can anyone besides the Savior keep all the
commandments all the time? If our only hope of inheriting
the celestial kingdom lies in keeping all the rules, obeying
all the commandments, and living all the principles perfectly, then you and I blew our chances long ago. It is true
that the gospel provides repentance, forgiveness, and atonement, but these are remedies for disobedience rather than
rewards for obedience.

Many members of the Church confuse the long-term
goal of individual perfection with the short-term necessity
of perfection-in-Christ, mistakenly concluding that they
must perfect themselves by their own efforts before they
have hope of receiving the kingdom of God. Elder Bruce R.
McConkie referred to this idea as one of the deadly heresies

of the modern Church.[3] If it were possible to perfect ourselves, to make ourselves worthy of the kingdom of God by our own efforts, we wouldn't need Jesus Christ at all: "I do not frustrate the grace of God: for if righteousness come by [keeping] the law, then Christ is dead in vain." (Gal. 2:21.) If we could be justified by our own efforts, then we wouldn't need a savior at all, and Christ's infinite sacrifice would have been all for nothing.

JUSTIFICATION BY FAITH IN CHRIST

The only other way of being justified, of being declared not guilty before God, is to admit our own imperfections, admit we can't be perfect on our own or save ourselves by our own efforts, and have faith in Christ our Savior. We must accept his offer of help by entering into a completely new covenant in which his efforts are added to our own and make up for our deficiencies. This is called justification by faith in Christ.

In the new covenant of faith, perfect innocence is still required, but it is required of the team or partnership of Christ-and-me, rather than of me alone. Because Christ and I are one in the gospel covenant, God accepts our combined total worthiness, and together Christ and I are perfectly worthy. As a result, in Christ I am clean and worthy today. My individual perfect performance remains a long-term personal goal and will be the eventual outcome of the covenant

---

[3]Bruce R. McConkie, "The Seven Deadly Heresies," in *Devotional Speeches of the Year* (Provo: BYU Press, 1980) pp. 74–80.

relationship, but it is not a prerequisite to being justified in the short run by faith in Christ. "We know that all men must repent and believe on the name of Jesus Christ, and worship the Father in his name, and endure in faith on his name to the end, or they cannot be saved in the kingdom of God. And we know that justification through the grace of our Lord and Savior Jesus Christ is just and true." (D&C 20:29–30.)

In the New Testament the two means of justification, by law and by faith, are referred to as separate yokes or burdens. The obligation of the law with its demand for perfect obedience was compared to a heavy "yoke of bondage" (Gal. 5:1; see Acts 15:10), while the obligations of the gospel covenant with its repentance, forgiveness, and atonement are called "easy" and "light": "Come unto me, all ye that labour and are heavy laden, and I will give you rest. Take my yoke upon you, and learn of me; for I am meek and lowly in heart: and ye shall find rest unto your souls. For my yoke is easy, and my burden is light." (Matt. 11:28–30.)

There is no heavier yoke than the demand for perfection—the curse of the law. And many of the Saints still struggle under its load. But the good news is that in Christ we are set free of that crushing burden. He bore that particular burden for us, and his perfect performance extended and applied to us frees us from a similar requirement at this time. In the gospel covenant, we exchange the burden of sin for the obligation to love him and each other and to do the very best we can.

KEEPING THE COMMANDMENTS

But are we not required then to keep the commandments? The answer is yes — and no. When I ask my students if it is necessary to keep the commandments to enter into the celestial kingdom, they all answer with absolute certainty that it is. They know that this is true because they have heard Church leaders and teachers tell them so all of their lives. But when I ask them if they've ever broken a commandment, or if they are not now living any commandments one hundred percent, most of them answer in the affirmative. They don't usually see the major problem implied by these two answers.

Latter-day Saints habitually use the phrase "keeping the commandments" differently from its technical and historical meaning outside the Church. This is not wrong, but it is different, and for this reason "keeping the commandments" is sometimes an ambiguous and troublesome phrase for the Latter-day Saints, particularly when they talk to non-Latter-day Saints. We generally say "keeping the commandments" when what we really mean is "trying real hard to keep the commandments and succeeding most of the time." Defined in this way, the phrase describes the *attempts* at obedience that the new covenant requires as our token of "good faith." Defined in this way, "keeping the commandments" is both possible and necessary; that is, *trying* to keep the commandments, doing the best we can at it, *is* a requirement of the gospel covenant, even though succeeding right now in keeping all of the commandments all of the time is not. This is why the gospel covenant offers repentance and atonement in addition to commandments.

Technically, however, this customary LDS usage is incorrect. If we insist on fine points, *"keeping* the commandments" means not breaking them—not any of them, not ever. It means keeping them perfectly, and in reality no one does this. Technically, you can't claim to keep the commandments in this sense so long as you break any of them at all. This is what James means when he says in James 2:10: "For whosoever shall keep the whole law, and yet offend in one point, he is guilty of all. For he that said, Do not commit adultery, said also, Do not kill. Now if thou commit no adultery, yet if thou kill, thou art become a transgressor of the law."

The ambiguity between the traditional meaning and the customary LDS usage of "keeping the commandments" has caused Latter-day Saints and other Christians to talk past each other on occasion and led some who don't understand our theological vocabulary to accuse us of believing in salvation by works. It has also caused some in the Church to conclude incorrectly that perfect performance is a requirement of the gospel covenant, even though the real bottom line is being committed to the proper goals and doing all we can to achieve them. In fact, the whole purpose of the atonement of Christ is to provide a way whereby those who have not kept, do not keep, and probably will not keep all the commandments all the time can still be exalted in the celestial kingdom of God—where they will continue to make progress in eternity until they are perfected — provided that they genuinely hunger and thirst after righteousness.

In the New Testament, when Paul talks about keeping the commandments or being justified by works, he means obeying all the commandments all the time. Therefore he rightly concludes that no one can "keep the commandments" in this sense, that our failure to keep the commandments perfectly condemns us, and that we must look somewhere else for a means of salvation. Strictly speaking, then, it doesn't matter which commandments you keep and which ones you break; if you don't keep them all, you are a transgressor and guilty rather than righteous or just. When the terms are defined in this way, clearly whoever would claim to be righteous on the basis of "keeping the commandments" must keep all of the commandments all of the time. Good luck.

THE TERMS OF THE NEW COVENANT

Where the terms of the old contract, the Mosaic law, were perfect obedience to rules in exchange for justification before God, salvation from enemies, and an inheritance in the promised land, the terms of the new contract are (1) faith in the Lord Jesus Christ — an ongoing belief in and commitment to the Savior, (2) repentance — an ongoing process of repudiating our mistakes and trying again, and (3) baptism — a symbolic ordinance in which the actual removal of guilt takes place. When we have done all this, we are worthy to (4) receive the gift of the Holy Ghost.

Receiving this gift verifies that the covenant is accepted,

that we have been cleansed of our past sins, and that we are therefore worthy of the companionship of this third member of the Godhead. (See 3 Ne. 27:19–21.) Those who keep the new covenant also receive justification before God, salvation from enemies (our *real* enemies — sin and death), and an inheritance in a promised land (the kingdom of God). Thus the new covenant provides for us, on terms we can meet, all the blessings promised by, but unattainable under, the old covenant.

So this is one way of understanding the gospel covenant, the Savior's proposition — his proposal to his beloved. The covenant is an agreement, a partnership agreement, between ourselves and our Savior. We must believe in Christ, and we must believe in justification by faith in Christ. We must be committed to both. Knowing that we cannot do everything that the law demanded from us, in the gospel covenant we agree to do all that we *can* do. We agree to give our Savior our best effort, to give him everything we have. We agree that perfection is our ultimate goal and that we will work with him toward that goal. Thus the idea of "keeping the commandments" is still a vital part of the arrangement, but "keeping the commandments *perfectly*" isn't, at least not for now. In return for this wonderful concession, we also agree to repent whenever and however we fail to keep the commandments perfectly and to try again, and again, and again, if necessary, and never to give up repenting and trying to be like him.

The Savior in turn agrees to cover our mistakes while we are learning and making progress. Although our private,

48

individual perfection comes later, long after this life is over, our partnership perfection, our perfection-in-Christ, is effective immediately. From the moment we enter into the covenant with him, our mistakes are covered—we are perfected in him provided only that we continue in the covenant relationship, that we "endure to the end." As we are rendered innocent, clean, and worthy by faith, repentance, and baptism, we are able to receive the gift of the Holy Ghost, which God gives to us as "earnest money" (see Eph. 1:14; 2 Cor. 1:22; 5:5), a sort of guarantee and down payment on the wonderful blessings we will inherit. In the gift of the Holy Ghost, Christ also provides his junior partners with a compass for better spiritual navigation, with the comfort of a testimony, and with the assurance that they have indeed been justified through his covenant.

Like tithing, the terms of this covenant are in one sense the same for everyone, yet in another sense different for each according to individual ability. The terms of the law of tithing are universal—one tenth of our increase annually. (See D&C 119:4.) Yet this same formula works out to a different dollar amount for each individual. The same is true of the gospel covenant. The Savior requires from each of us a specific percentage: all that we have, or one hundred percent. Yet each individual's one hundred percent will be a different quantity from everyone else's, depending on the spiritual knowledge and maturity of the individual. What a marvelous flexibility—he never requires more than I am able to give, and what he does require of me is always appropriate to my knowledge and circumstances.

This is why I mustn't be discouraged that I haven't made as much progress as Brother X or Sister Y. My obligation is to give all *I* have, not all someone else has, to be as good as *I* can be, not as good as someone else is. In Doctrine and Covenants 10:4 the Lord even warns against running faster than we are able: "Do not run faster or labor more than you have strength and means provided." Have faith in Christ; do the best you can; don't try to do more than you can.

The apostles and prophets are justified through faith in Christ on exactly the same terms as I am, and when I reach their level of growth and maturity in the gospel, their level of performance will be required of me—but not until then. So I should not despair just because I don't seem to be doing as well as some others are doing, just as I should not expect to pay the same quantity in tithing as some others pay. What God requires in both cases is fair and appropriate for each individual.

However, the converse is also true. Just as I shouldn't get depressed because some do better than I do, even so I shouldn't look down on those who don't do as well as I do. For the terms of the contract are the same for them as for me: "Give me all you have, however great or small a quantity that may be, and I will do the rest while you learn how." No matter that we have sixty-one cents, or a dollar and a half, or two cents—the bargain is the same: "Give me all you have, and I will do the rest." Since we are all short of what we need, though by differing amounts, we are all in the same boat and in need of the same salvation. Therefore, the Savior's covenant offer is the same to all.

ATTITUDE

Obviously then, the crucial consideration for determining whether or not we have a valid covenant is not necessarily our relative performance or even our "goodness" as we humans judge goodness, but rather our attitude—the desires of our heart. The scriptures themselves make this clear: "Wherefore, redemption cometh in and through the Holy Messiah; for he is full of grace and truth. Behold he offereth himself a sacrifice for sin, to answer the ends of the law, unto all those who have a broken heart and a contrite spirit; and unto none else can the ends of the law be answered." (2 Ne. 2:6–7.)

Attitude—the condition of our hearts—is everything. No matter how proud we may be of our relative ability to keep the commandments, until our attitude is right, until our hearts are broken and our spirits are contrite, our relative goodness is of little benefit. However impressive any individual's relative performance might be, without the Savior that performance is insufficient for salvation; it falls short of the celestial perfection required for the presence of God.

On the other hand, once our attitude is right—that is, once our hearts are broken and our spirits are contrite—our relative weakness is of just as little importance, provided we enter into and keep the covenant. When the cost of the bicycle is over one hundred dollars, what possible difference can it make in the long run that I lacked one hundred but you lacked only ninety-nine? We are both beggars at the mercy of God. Therefore, I can feel no superiority over the least struggling member. I can only feel empathy for someone who shares my own situation before God.

THE SACRAMENT

Because conversion and repentance are not once-and-for-all events, and because we cannot keep all the commandments all the time, the covenant must be renewed and reaffirmed on a regular basis. Fallen beings like ourselves need to be reminded of the covenant we made and the commitment we expressed at baptism. We need frequent opportunities for course corrections. In many denominations, it would be thought odd that the sacrament of the Lord's Supper is offered every week. Yet Latter-day Saints know that imperfect beings must regularly reaffirm their personal goal of perfection, being justified in the meantime by the atonement of Christ.

Accordingly, each week we come before the Lord as we prepare for the sacrament and say essentially, "Heavenly Father, I wasn't perfect again this week, but I repent of my sins and reaffirm my commitment to keep all the commandments. I promise to go back and try again with all my heart, might, mind, and strength. I still want and need the cleansing that comes through faith, repentance, and baptism. Please extend my contract, my covenant of baptism, and grant me the continued blessings of the Atonement and the companionship of the Holy Ghost."

Doctrine and Covenants 20:77 may be the scripture

most familiar to Latter-day Saints. This prayer is offered every time the Saints renew their covenant relationship with God: "O God, the Eternal Father, we ask thee in the name of thy Son, Jesus Christ, to bless and sanctify this bread to the souls of all those who partake of it, that they may eat in remembrance of the body of thy Son, and witness unto thee, O God, the Eternal Father . . . "

As we renew the gospel covenant by partaking of the sacrament, we naturally must do it in remembrance of the Son who made the covenant possible. Then with our Savior and his sacrifice in mind, we bear witness of certain things. To witness means to testify, to swear to, or to affirm. Hence, "and witness unto thee" introduces the specific affirmations, the legal fine print, of the prayer: " . . . and witness unto thee, O God, the Eternal Father, that they *are willing to* take upon them the name of thy Son, and always remember him and keep his commandments which he has given them." (Italics added.)

Why are the three words "are willing to" necessary here? Are they important? Would it make a difference if the prayer left these out and just read: " . . . and witness unto thee, O God, the Eternal Father, that they take upon them the name of thy Son, and always remember him and keep his commandments which he has given them"? Yes, it would make a difference. It would make a difference because I cannot do this latter thing. I can't witness, affirm, or swear that I *do* always remember him and keep his commandments. I would be lying, and I know it—I want to do the right thing, but sometimes I don't. This is precisely the problem that makes the atonement of Christ and the gospel covenant necessary for me in the first place—I can't keep all the commandments all the time no matter how hard I try. It follows that I can't honestly witness to God that I *will* keep all the commandments when I know that, in some degree at least, I probably won't.

However, I can with absolute honesty witness that I *am willing to*. I can swear that this is the desire of my heart. I can affirm that I hunger and thirst after these things, that I will do all I can to be obedient. Thus even by the technical terms of the covenant renewal prayer, God lets me know that the honest commitment of my heart and my best efforts are sufficient for the covenant to be renewed, and that the covenant of faith is sufficient, through the grace of Christ, to justify me before God.

THE ACCEPTABILITY OF COMMITTED HEARTS

Above all else, God wants our hearts. Imperfect performance can be corrected, sins can be remitted, mistakes can be erased—but God can do nothing with an unwilling and rebellious heart until it repents. Weakness can be saved; rebellion cannot. "Behold, the Lord requireth the heart and a willing mind." (D&C 64:34.)

Another scripture that indicates how our sincere willingness and honest desire are acceptable to God in the absence of perfect performance is Doctrine and Covenants 46:9. This scripture deals with the gifts of the Spirit enjoyed by the Saints: "They are given for the benefit of those who love me and keep all my commandments, . . . " The gifts of the Spirit are for those who love God and keep *all* his commandments? Oh, no—not *all* the commandments! I'll never qualify! But wait, there's a comma! " . . . *and* him that *seeketh* so to do." (Italics added.) Thank God for what comes after the comma! Even those of us who aren't perfect may enjoy the gifts and blessings of the Spirit, as long as we are seeking to keep the commandments to the best of our ability.

Similarly, it is recorded in the Pearl of Great Price how the Holy Ghost confirmed to Adam "that as thou hast fallen thou mayest be redeemed, and all mankind, even as many as will." (Moses 5:9.) Notice that it doesn't say, "Even as many as are perfect." The point is clear: Adam is *not* perfect; Adam is imperfect and fallen (like you and me). That's why he needed a Savior (like you and me). The promise is to as many as *will* (using "will" in the older sense of "to be willing")—thus, to all those who really want redemption from their imperfection. Another of the great promises of the new covenant is that all those who really want and work for the kingdom of God with all their strength, however great or little their strength may be, will inherit that kingdom.

And that is good news.

Chapter Four

SAVED BY GRACE

I often ask my students the following question, "When you stand before the bar of God at the Judgment Day, how many of you would like the assurance that God will be absolutely fair with you?" Usually every hand goes up. Then I pull the rug out from under them. "You'd better think again. To be fair means to judge you by the law of justice and to give you what you deserve. But imperfect and fallen mortals like ourselves don't want to get what we deserve; we should be hoping for more than that. We don't want God to be fair or just when he judges us—we want him to be *merciful*." The atonement of Christ provides a way for God to be at the same time both just and merciful. Since Christ and I are one in the gospel covenant, and since in a covenant partnership it doesn't matter which partner does what, Christ can answer the demands of justice for me, and I can then receive the benefits of mercy from him. This is an arrangement that satisfies both justice and mercy.

Yet some people are so addicted to the law of justice that they have difficulty accommodating the law of mercy or grace. They chafe at certain aspects of the gospel and of mercy that seem to them unfair (in other words, merciful rather than just). For example, it really *isn't* fair that one person should suffer for the sins of others. It isn't fair that some people can commit horrible crimes and then be completely forgiven and cleansed without having to suffer for them. It isn't fair that those who labor for only an hour will get the same reward as those who labor all day. (See Matt. 20:1–16.) No, the gospel sometimes isn't fair, but that is actually part of the good news. It isn't fair—it's merciful, and thank God it is so, for no human being can stand acquitted before the demands of absolute justice. From the perspective of fallen, imperfect mortals like ourselves, being judged by justice alone is our worst nightmare.

Nevertheless, some of us can't seem to turn loose of the law of justice. I have had many people say to me, "Well, what you say about mercy and grace would be wonderful, if it were true, but it doesn't feel right to me. It's too easy— it doesn't seem fair." In other words, "I can't accept mercy because it doesn't feel like justice." But that is precisely the point—precisely the good news. The gospel offers mercy to those who would otherwise be damned by justice. What do the scriptures say? "O the greatness of the *mercy* of our God, the Holy One of Israel! For he delivereth his saints from that awful monster the devil, and death, and hell, and that lake of fire and brimstone, which is endless torment." (2 Ne 9:19; italics added.)

Now it is not an *unfair* or *unjust* fate that the Saints are to be delivered from. There is nothing *wrong* with people going to hell—they deserve it. After all, they incurred an honest debt of sin, and paying it is only right: "Wo unto him that has the law given, yea, that has all the commandments of God, like unto us, and that transgresseth them, and that wasteth the days of his probation, for awful is his state!" (2 Ne. 9:27.) In the situation described in these two scriptures, the devil, death, and hell receive power over individuals only to the extent and duration that are warranted for the payment of individual debts. Hell is not a satanic invention—it is part of *God's* plan, and it is perfectly just and fair. It is true that Satan rules there, but only at the sufferance of God. The threat of hell is the threat of getting justice, of getting what we deserve and of paying what we owe without any interference from mercy.

On the other hand, the atonement of Christ offers a way to receive mercy instead of justice and to avoid a just punishment in hell. Nevertheless, if we reject the mercy offered by Christ, then suffering for our sins is right and just and fair. Justice could never intervene to save us from a *just* punishment—only mercy can do that. "While his arm of mercy is extended towards you in the light of the day, harden not your hearts. . . . [Otherwise,] according to the power of justice, for justice cannot be denied, ye must go away into that lake of fire and brimstone, whose flames are unquenchable, and whose smoke ascendeth up forever and ever, which lake of fire and brimstone is endless torment." (Jacob 6:5, 10.)

In this life there are only two lords and two sides. We must choose to belong to the One or the other. If we do not choose the One, we will receive the other by default. There is no middle ground, no third alternative. Life, like a computer, has default settings, conditions that will automatically apply unless we take positive action to avoid them. Thus, if we refuse to make Christ our Lord by taking positive steps to enter into his covenant, then Satan becomes our lord by default. Christ by choice or Satan by default—there are no other options.

Christ "shall bring salvation to all those who shall believe on his name; this being the intent of this last sacrifice, to bring about the bowels of mercy, which overpowereth justice, and bringeth about means unto men that they may have faith unto repentance. And thus mercy can satisfy the demands of justice, and encircles them in the arms of safety." (Alma 34:15–16.) The choice before us is mercy or justice. Either choice can be accommodated, and either choice is compatible with the nature and plan of God, but, as in the choice between the Lord and Satan, there are no third alternatives. Again, life has default settings, and they are set for justice. We can choose the mercy that is offered through the gospel covenant, but if we refuse that mercy, we will receive justice.

Now here is an odd thing about the nature of mercy: by definition, mercy can only be mercy if we *don't* deserve it. For if we deserve something, then it becomes a matter of justice that we receive it. So it ceases to be a matter of mercy. Thus, in this sense at least, to give or to receive mercy is always somewhat unfair. But one of the great beauties of the gospel, some of the best news of all, is that Jesus Christ does not mind this unfairness. He is willing to suffer unfairly and compensate justice himself out of his own person in order to extend mercy to weaker beings like us. This willingness on his part to pay more than his fair share and to carry more than his fair load in order to grant mercy to others constitutes the grace of Christ.

GRACE

In the King James Bible, the English word *grace* has several different meanings. The Hebrew or Greek words usually translated "grace" (*hen* or *charis*, respectively) are also translated as favor, pleasure, thanks, graciousness, or goodwill. The term is also used for a gift, benefit, or gesture offered in token of these attitudes. In contemporary society, a tip or gratuity (from the same Latin root as *grace*) represents much the same thing. A customer pays his bill—that is what justice demands—but the tip is based on goodwill. There is no obligation. Grace in the King James Bible can also mean comeliness or beauty (James 1:11), or it can mean the favor or special status one person grants to another in return for good service (see Gen. 33:8), for spiritual merit (see 1 Sam. 2:18), or even for physical beauty (see Esth. 2:15–17).

However, in the New Testament, "grace" most often refers to the grace or favor of God, and this is usually understood as an attitude of goodwill that predisposes God to act positively toward human beings. The operative word here is *pre*disposes. In other words, before I have a track record, before I can be cute or smart or charming or even righteous, before I can earn any rewards or deserve any blessings— *before* all this—God is already *pre*disposed positively toward me. Grace in this sense is not something that I can trigger, manipulate, earn, deserve, or control, for it is a preexisting aspect of God's attitude toward me. Before I could even respond to him, he already loved me, wanted to help me, and wanted me to succeed. (Cf. 1 Jn. 4:19.) Because of this predisposition in my favor, God also grants me gifts from time to time to help me succeed. Such gifts are also referred to in scripture occasionally as the grace of God, since they are tokens of his positive predisposition toward me.

Like our Heavenly Father, most parents are predisposed positively toward their children even before the child does anything to return the favor. Even when all a child can do is cry and wet its pants, even then it can usually draw on a vast reservoir of parental love and care and concern. Though children consume much more than they produce, most parents are predisposed to treat them with favor, or in other words to grant them grace. Thus, they do things for their children that they might not do for other people.

Later on, the child's entreaty "Please!" is an appeal to that parental grace, to mom or dad's goodwill and favor. "Please!" isn't an argument; it presents no evidence that what is requested is just or deserved. It does not imply that the object in mind has been earned. It merely says, "Do it because you love me and are predisposed in my favor, or do it simply because I want or need it, and you care about my wants and needs. Do it as a sign of your favor, as an expression of your affection for me. Do it because we belong to each other." The Spanish term for *please*, "por favor," which means literally "for the sake of grace (or favor)," preserves the true nature of the entreaty "please!"

Theologically, the grace of God is his goodwill toward us, his predisposition to act in our best interest even before we can earn or deserve such consideration. Latter-day Saints understand that God's unconditional grace has been expressed to his children in many ways. For example, God made us his own spirit children in a premortal life. This was a great blessing, yet we did not ask for it, and there was no way we could deserve or earn it or claim a right to it in advance of his making us his children. God did it because he had the ability to do it and because we would be better off if he did. Our birth as his spirit children was an unearned expression of our Father's goodwill — of unprovoked and indiscriminate love and caring. This is pure grace. Moreover, just as parents love their tiny infants even before they can respond to that love, so God loved us even before we had the ability to love him back, let alone "earn" his love with good behavior.

God's grace is also extended to and claims children who die before the age of accountability. (See D&C 29:46; 137:10.) Likewise, it claims the mentally handicapped (see D&C 29:50)[1] and those who are genuinely ignorant of God's

---

[1] See Calvin P. Rudd, "Salvation of Children," in *Encyclopedia of Mormonism*, ed. Daniel H. Ludlow (New York: Macmillan Publishing Company, 1992), 1:269.

commandments to the extent of their ignorance (see 2 Ne. 9:25–26). In all such cases, God is predisposed to act unilaterally in their favor without any performance on their part that earns his concern. They are saved by grace. Latter-day Saints also believe that God removed the sin of Adam (or original sin) from Adam's posterity by and through his grace, as a unilateral act of goodwill. (See Moro. 8:8.) Thus all human beings will be resurrected through the grace of God. These aspects of the grace of God are gifts we can neither manipulate nor earn.

Nevertheless, the term *grace* is sometimes used in a different sense to describe a quality that *is* responsive or reactive to human behavior. When spoken of in this sense, God's favor or grace is not a preexisting given but is something that can be sought after, increased, decreased, or even lost completely by an individual's own actions. Thus Peter can insist in 1 Peter 5:5 that God gives grace to the humble (as opposed to those who lack humility). He also exhorts believers to "*grow* in grace." (See 2 Pet. 3:18; italics added. Cf. Luke 2:52.) John explains that believers receive grace for grace, or in other words they receive increased favor from God as they react positively (graciously) to grace already received. (See John 1:16; see also D&C 93:12, 19–20.) Paul even warns the Galatians against falling from grace through their own foolishness. (See Gal. 1:6; 5:4.)

This reactive or responsive grace can "be multiplied" (e.g., 1 Pet. 1:2), it "abounds" under certain circumstances, and it can be received "in vain" (2 Cor. 6:1). It is used in the sense of reward in Luke 6:32–34 ("What thank have ye?")[2] and of the thanks that humans owe God. Thus even now, "to say grace" means to offer the thanks due to God in return for his blessings. This responsive kind of grace is also the nuance behind most of the scriptural passages in which one individual speaks of finding "grace in the eyes of" another. (See, e.g., Gen. 19:19; 1 Sam. 20:3.) When the term *grace* is used with this nuance, as responsive grace, we see how an individual can be said to grow from grace to grace until ultimately coming to a "fulness of grace." (D&C 93:13, 19–20.)

Thus we see that some aspects of God's favor or grace are unilateral and without preconditions. These things God has already done for us without any consideration of our individual behavior. They are sheer gifts granted to all human beings alike out of his preexisting love for us. However, other aspects of God's favor or grace are conditional and may increase, decrease, or even cease altogether in our lives depending upon how we respond to their influence. Nevertheless, in both cases love and grace flow from God to human beings — they originate in him as part of his nature, and he makes the first move. God loves us not because we're so lovable he can't help himself — he loves us because his nature is loving, because God *is* love. (See 1 Jn. 4:8.)

SAVED BY GRACE

The greatest expression of God's love and of his unilateral and unconditional grace is in his providing a Savior

---

[2]The Greek word *charis*, translated here as "thank," is the standard New Testament word for "grace."

for those who sin. "For God so loved the world, that he gave his only begotten Son, that whosoever believeth in him should not perish, but have everlasting life." (John 3:16.) The atonement of Christ and its offer of mercy are there for us whether we are righteous or not, whether we deserve it or not. It is offered alike to the wicked and the just (relatively speaking). Everyone has been invited to receive it. This solution to all life's problems has been provided *gratis* (by grace). Justice did not require that the Father provide a Savior, nor did justice require that Jesus Christ offer to be that Savior and suffer in our place to redeem us. When he saw our weakness, our peril, and our need, his love and compassion for us moved him to offer his intervention – to volunteer.

The gospel covenant is therefore a covenant of grace, an expression of God's goodwill. God didn't have to offer this new covenant to us, and Christ didn't have to volunteer for the assignment. We humans did not earn or merit the offer of a new covenant. Quite the opposite: the gospel covenant was only necessary in the first place because of our *dis*-obedience and our *in*ability to keep the commandments. We didn't *earn* it – we *needed* it. No grace, no volunteer; no volunteer, no savior; no savior, no salvation. The conclusion is inescapable – we *are* saved by grace.

For some reason, however, some Latter-day Saints are uneasy about the doctrine of grace. I believe this is because they have been so turned off by certain non-LDS interpretations of grace that they have rejected the term altogether, thus throwing out the baby with the bath water. However, given the number of places in the LDS scriptures where the doctrine of grace is taught, we cannot deny its central place in the gospel. Consider for example, the following passages from the Book of Mormon:

> Reconcile yourselves to the will of God, and not to the will of the devil and the flesh; and remember, after ye are reconciled unto God, that it is only in and through the grace of God that ye are saved. (2 Ne. 10:24.)

> We labor diligently to write, to persuade our children, and also our brethren, to believe in Christ, and to be reconciled to God; for we know that it is by grace that we are saved, after all we can do. (2 Ne. 25:23.)

> If men come unto me I will show unto them their weakness. I give unto men weakness that they may be humble; and my grace is sufficient for all men that humble themselves before me; for if they humble themselves before me, and have faith in me, then will I make weak things become strong unto them. (Ether 12:27.)

> Come unto Christ, and be perfected in him, and deny yourselves of all ungodliness; and if ye shall deny yourselves of all ungodliness, and love God with all your might, mind and strength, then is his grace sufficient for you, that by his grace ye may be perfect in Christ; and if by the grace of God ye are perfect in Christ, ye can in nowise deny the power of God. And again, if ye by the grace of God are perfect in Christ, and deny not his power, then are ye sanctified in Christ by the grace of God, through the shedding of the blood

of Christ, which is in the covenant of the Father
unto the remission of your sins, that ye become
holy, without spot. (Moro. 10:32–33.)

However, for Latter-day Saints the doctrine of grace does
not mean that we are saved by grace *alone*, that is, without
participating in the process in some degree, nor does it mean
that salvation is totally without conditions. If that were true,
salvation would be something that just fell out of the sky
and happened to us—like getting struck by lightning or winning the lottery. The Latter-day Saints do not believe that
grace is either random or irresistible, or that salvation is a
unilateral decision on God's part (predestination). God may
be predisposed in our favor, he may put within our reach
what was once beyond us, and he may remove every obstacle
in the way of our salvation, but he will not force us down
the path he has cleared, nor will he save us without our
consent. The gospel covenant is provided by sheer grace,
but it must be entered into by choice.

Some theologians have suggested that any conditions
attached to grace would destroy its character as grace, but
I disagree. Suppose a dear relative offered you an all-expense-
paid trip to Hawaii *gratis* (i.e., by grace) and asked that you
respond to the invitation by a certain date. Would the required condition of an affirmative response make the offered
trip any less an act of goodwill and favor based on love?
Would you argue that once you responded affirmatively,
your relative then *owed* you the trip, that you had in fact
earned it by meeting the only condition placed on it—by
accepting the offer within the specified time? Does being

required to acknowledge a gift and affirm our desire to receive it change it from a gift to a wage?

Of course not, and in much the same way, God, our rich Heavenly Relative, offers us his kingdom by grace, by doing for us what we can't do for ourselves. But he also requires that we acknowledge and accept the offer by faith in Christ, repentance, baptism, and receiving the Holy Ghost. Then as long as we keep the gospel covenant, the grace of Jesus Christ is "sufficient to own, to redeem, and to justify."[3] The scriptures are clear—as long as we keep the covenant, the grace of Christ is not simply necessary, but *sufficient* for our salvation. (See Ether 12:27; Moro. 10:32–33.)

But we must agree to this arrangement. When we accept Christ and enter into his covenant, the demands of justice, which are demands for a perfection we do not have, are met by the grace of God, and we are saved. Thus the saving principles of the gospel covenant are offered to us as a favor, as an act of grace and goodwill. But we can still refuse grace. We can resist God's love and reject his covenant. Christ stands at the door and knocks, but he never kicks it in. We must open the door.

FAITH VS. WORKS

For centuries theologians have argued pointlessly over whether individuals are saved by faith or saved by works.

---

[3]"I Stand All Amazed," *Hymns* (Salt Lake City: The Church of Jesus Christ of Latter-day Saints, 1985), no. 193.

A pox on both their houses, for neither by faith alone (defining faith as mere passive belief)[4] nor by works alone are we saved. Salvation comes through a covenant relationship in which both faith and works play their parts. To insist that salvation comes by works alone, that we can earn it ourselves without needing the grace of God, insults the mercy of God and mocks the sacrifice of Jesus Christ in our behalf. On the other hand, to insist that salvation comes by belief alone and that God places no other obligations upon the believer insults the justice of God and makes Christ the minister of sin.

The scriptural concept of the covenant, an agreement between mortals and God that lays obligations on both parties and that satisfies both justice and mercy, eliminates the false either/or of faith versus works. In simple terms this is the arrangement – we do what we are able to do, and Jesus Christ, the object of our faith, out of his love and mercy and grace, does what we are not yet able to do. And we must believe he can do it – we must believe Christ.

In the parable of the talents, it did not matter that he with five talents earned five more while he with two talents earned only two. The efforts of both were accepted, though one had more talents and produced more results than the other. Indeed, even he with only one talent would have been accepted, if only he had done what he could – but he chose not to try.

---

[4]Several places in scripture define faith as "commitment," thus including in the single word *faith* both belief and behavior. In this special sense, it could be said that we are saved by faith alone (i.e., by a total commitment – by our belief and our behavior).

It is true that we cannot save ourselves by our works, but we can contribute something to the joint efforts of the partnership. To be in partnership, to be in a covenant relationship, we *must* do something. Even though our best efforts may be insufficient to save ourselves, they are sufficient as a token of good faith to establish a covenant with our Savior. Though that covenant relationship is then "sufficient to own, to redeem, and to justify," God still requires our participation. Without our assent and our participation, salvation would amount to nothing more than predestination, a happy accident that arbitrarily happens to some people and not to others.

No, we must participate in our own salvation to the extent that we are able. It is a partnership after all, and the junior partners must contribute what they can. To refuse such participation is to refuse the very idea of partnership. Two persons riding a tandem bicycle may not do the same amount of work, but if the weaker one uses that as an excuse to pull up his feet and stop pedaling altogether, then by definition the arrangement ceases to be a partnership and becomes exploitation. In the language of the gospel, it violates the covenant.

Trying our hardest to keep the commandments and be like Christ is part of our covenant obligation, not because we can succeed at them in this life, but because the attempt, the commitment to try, demonstrates *our* sincerity and our commitment to the covenant; it is a statement of our goals and desires. Our valiant attempts show that we really do hunger and thirst after righteousness — even if we don't always succeed at it. Faith is always willing to try—and to try again and again. While success is not a requirement of the covenant of faith, my best attempts are. The gospel covenant requires this "good faith" effort.

So the old debate about faith versus works is a false dichotomy, a phony either/or. No matter which side we choose, faith alone or works alone, we destroy the concept of a covenant, of the partnership between the individual and God.

RESISTING GRACE

Too many of us are saying to ourselves, "When I've done it, when I've perfected myself, when I've made myself completely righteous, then I'll be worthy of the Atonement. Then Christ can do his work and exalt me." But this will never happen, for it puts the cart before the horse. It's like saying, "When my tumor is gone, then I'll call the doctor. I'll be ready for him then." This is not how things are designed to work either in medicine or in the gospel. "They that be whole need not a physician, but they that are sick." (Matt. 9:12.)

Even a prophet as great as Moses learned that he could not stand against the power of Satan or cast him out until he tapped the power of God through the name of the Only Begotten. (See Moses 1:20–21.) Similarly, John saw that those who will receive salvation, strength, and the kingdom overcome Satan by the blood of the Lamb rather than through their own efforts. (See Rev. 12:10.)

I feel very strongly that in most cases the belief that we

must save ourselves by our own good works is not merely misinformed, it is evil. It is evil in the first place because it places an impossible burden on people—the burden of being perfect. Eventually they will despair and give up. Second, it is evil because it keeps people from admitting their need of a savior and accepting the merits and mercy of the Holy Messiah. It keeps them from understanding Jesus Christ in his role as Savior. Finally, it is evil because some people are simply too arrogant to admit their own imperfection. They refuse to think of themselves as sinners or to admit there is anything they can't do on their own. Such hearts will not break—they are too proud. These individuals think of Christ and his atonement merely as handy tools to be used in saving themselves, just as a carpenter would use a hammer and nails to build a house. The emphasis, and the credit, is on themselves as do-it-yourself saviors rather than on Christ. No carpenter thanks his hammer.

No one who thinks he can work out his own salvation[5] has the necessary humility to receive the cleansing of Christ's atonement: "He offereth himself a sacrifice for sin, to answer the ends of the law, unto all those who have a broken heart and a contrite spirit; and unto none else can the ends of the law be answered." (2 Ne. 2:7.)

This is precisely the point the Savior makes in the par-

---

[5]In Philippians 2:12 ("work out your own salvation with fear and trembling"), Paul did *not* teach that we can save ourselves. He of all people knew better. Rather he meant, as the next verse explicitly states, that while we may do the work, God is the one working in us, with us, and through us both to desire and to accomplish the common goal of our salvation. Both our work and God's grace are necessary.

able of the Pharisee and the publican. (See Luke 18:9–14.) The Pharisee was one of those who "trusted in themselves that they were righteous." (V. 9.) The publican on the other hand did not do as well as the Pharisee at keeping all the commandments of God—but he knew it, and his heart was broken because of it. Now many who read this parable want to make the Pharisee out to be a hypocrite, but the text offers no evidence of this. The Pharisee really *did* do all the things he felt proud and superior about, and the publican really didn't. But that's not the point. This parable is not about hypocrisy; it's about *pride.* By objective human standards, in terms of the number and frequency of rules kept, the Pharisee really *was* the more righteous of the two individuals! Yet according to the Savior: "I tell you, this man [the publican] went down to his house justified rather than the other [the Pharisee]: for every one that exalteth himself shall be abased; and he that humbleth himself shall be exalted." (V. 14.)

I fear that, like the Pharisee in the parable, some of us who are relatively good at keeping the rules also trust in ourselves that we are righteous. Such are inordinately proud of their own goodness; they exalt themselves. But whenever we are proud of how good we are instead of being humbled by how imperfect we are (cf. 2 Ne. 4:17–19), our hearts are not broken, nor are our spirits contrite.

I remember a missionary we knew in the East who simply could not be instructed on this subject. He once said, "Of course I can make myself perfect. That's the difference between Latter-day Saints and other Christians. They think they are saved by grace, that God hands them everything on a silver platter, and we know that we have to do it all ourselves, that we have to make ourselves perfect. I'm very good at what I do already, and I'm confident that I will have made myself perfect by the time I'm thirty or so." He would be over thirty now. I have often wondered how he's doing.

Whose merit is it that gets us to the kingdom? Whose good works make us perfect? Even those scriptures peculiar to the Latter-day Saints are clear on this matter:

> Since man had fallen *he could not merit anything of himself;* but the sufferings and death of Christ atone for their sins, through faith and repentance, and so forth. (Alma 22:14; italics added.)

> I also thank my God, yea, my great God, that he hath granted unto us that we might repent of these things, and also that he hath forgiven us of those our many sins and murders which we have committed, and taken away the guilt from our hearts, *through the merits of his Son.* (Alma 24:10; italics added.)

> . . . *relying alone upon the merits of Christ,* who was the author and the finisher of their faith. (Moro. 6:4; italics added.)

> . . . that they might know the promises of the Lord, and that they may believe the gospel and *rely upon the merits of Jesus Christ,* and be glorified through faith in his name, and that through their repentance they might be saved. (D&C 3:20; italics added.)

Those who plan to enter the kingdom of God on their own merits do not yet understand how perfection comes or where the credit for it must go. They glorify their own efforts and attribute to themselves the role of savior. Moreover, the Prophet Zenock warns us in the Book of Mormon that we may incur the anger of God by failing to appreciate his mercy and grace: "Thou art angry, O Lord, with this people, because they will not understand thy mercies which thou hast bestowed upon them because of thy Son." (Alma 33:16.)

Of course the archetype for those who want to exalt themselves and take credit for what only the Savior can do is Satan himself. In Moses 4:1 we are told that Satan insisted, "Surely I will do it; wherefore give me thine honor." I suggest that those who fail to appreciate their utter dependence upon the Savior and who insist they are working out their own salvation are guilty of this same satanic attitude. Much better to be the sinful publican relying in humility upon the mercy of God than the self-righteous Pharisee trusting in his own good works to save him, for the former at least has learned that he needs a Savior and is ready to accept him and repent, while the latter has not. (Of course, an even better alternative would be to combine the broken heart and humility of the publican with the obedience of the Pharisee.)

MY YOKE IS EASY

Some people reject the idea of grace because it seems too easy. They *want* being saved to be harder than it is. There is a certain comfort in saying, "Salvation is so hard that I couldn't possibly make it, so I don't really need to try." This provides a convenient excuse for not trying at all. This reminds me a little bit of the young woman who kept turning down a date from a man who just as persistently shot her excuses down one by one. Finally she was forced to admit the truth, "Look, I'm all out of excuses, so I'll give it to you straight. I just don't want to go out with you."

Some of us try similar evasive tactics with the Lord when he invites us into his kingdom. We give excuse after excuse why we can't enter in. But God's grace, which has removed all the obstacles and cleared the path, shoots down all our excuses. By his grace any problem can be overcome, any circumstances can be worked around, anyone can be saved—if only we just really want the kingdom. We say, "I'd really like to go with you, but I can't keep this or that commandment all the time," and he replies, "Can you keep it ninety percent of the time (or eighty or seventy)? Then start there for now, and we'll work on it together!" Finally, in the face of all God has done and is willing to do for us, after he has cleared away all the obstacles and we are faced with an open door, we must either say, "Yes, I want to go with you," or "Look, I'll give it to you straight, I just don't want to go." None of us can weasel our way out by saying, "I'd really like to, but I can't." Grace has eliminated every excuse but one: "I just don't want to go; I prefer my sins to your kingdom."

Whenever I hear someone complain that the doctrine of grace makes things too easy, I think of the occasion when the Lord tried to illustrate the grace, merit, and mercy of

Christ to Israel when they had sinned in the wilderness: "He did straiten them in the wilderness with his rod; for they hardened their hearts, even as ye have; and the Lord straitened them because of their iniquity. He sent fiery flying serpents among them; and after they were bitten he prepared a way that they might be healed; and the labor which they had to perform was to look; and because of the simpleness of the way, or the easiness of it, there were many who perished." (1 Ne. 17:41; cf. Num 21:4–9; Alma 33:20.)

I fear that in the modern Church we similarly have those who will perish rather than accept the grace of God because it seems to them too easy. They will not believe Christ. But as Alma said to his son Helaman: "Do not let us be slothful because of the easiness of the way; for so was it with our fathers; for so was it prepared for them, that if they would look they might live; even so it is with us. The way is prepared, and if we will look we may live forever." (Alma 37:46.)

The Old Testament story of Naaman the leper also warns against dismissing the simple mercies of God. Naaman came to the prophet Elisha, desiring to be healed and expecting the cure to be both difficult and expensive. When Elisha told him to go bathe in the Jordan seven times, "he turned and went away in a rage" (1 Kgs. 5:12), feeling insulted and put off by so simple a prescription. Fortunately his servants were able to convince him to give the "too easy" remedy a try. "If the prophet had bid thee do some great thing, wouldest thou not have done it? how much rather then, when he saith to thee, Wash, and be clean?" (1 Kgs. 5:13.)

And Naaman humbled himself, did the simple thing he was asked to do, and was healed. Was Naaman in his rage any different from those of us today who think the waters of baptism and the grace of God are too "easy" to cleanse us of our sins? When Peter said, "Depart from me; for I am a sinful man, O Lord," he was probably telling the truth. But apparently Jesus found some small use for him anyway.

My colleague Leon Hartshorn relates a poignant story about how his father's belief in Christ was increased:

> My father was a good man. He took good care of my mother for numerous years while she was ill before she passed away. He taught his children to be honest and upright. He always paid his tithing, but he did not attend Church. My father had worked in the mines much of his life, in an environment that did not usually invite the Spirit of God, and perhaps for this reason he did not think that he could be fully active and enjoy the full blessings of activity in the gospel.
>
> When I had been married two or three years, I returned to my father's home for a visit. As we sat down together, he said to me, "Son, I've had a dream. I dreamed I was standing on the edge of a cliff, and the Savior came riding toward me on a horse. He had a rope tied to the saddle and wrapped around the saddle horn. He reached the rope out to me and said, 'Bob, I want you to lower me and my horse down this cliff.' I replied that this was impossible; there was no way one man could lower the weight of a horse and rider down

a cliff. He responded, 'Bob, lower me and my horse down the cliff.' So I took the end of the rope and lowered them down the cliff. To my surprise, it was not difficult at all. When the horse and rider arrived at the bottom of the cliff, he looked up and said, 'Bob, drop the rope.' I dropped it, and he wound it around the saddle horn again. Then looking up at me from the bottom of the cliff, he said simply, 'Bob, it's just that easy for you to live my commandments if you will try.' " It was a lesson my father could understand, a lesson in his own language of horses, riders, saddles, and ropes. Thereafter he would try whatever he was asked to do in the Church and was very active during the last twenty-five years of his life.

SOME FRUITS OF GRACE

There is transforming power in the grace of Christ for those whose hearts break in humble acknowledgment of their need for grace and mercy. I knew a member of the Church once whose sense of justice was so strong that he couldn't accept the atonement of Christ, although he did not realize it at the time. Oh, he was a hard man—hard on his wife and kids, hard on his friends and neighbors, and most of all hard on himself. He was never really unfair, but he seldom forgave, and he *never* forgot. He strove for absolute perfection in all that he did, and he was absolutely intolerant of failure and of those who failed. To him a "nice try" or a "valiant effort" were just euphemisms for failure, and heaven help his wife or his children if they failed to meet his expectations! In all fairness, this man never asked anyone else for a break, but he never gave one either. To him the idea that we could be forgiven of our sins because of what Christ had done and thereby totally escape paying a just penalty seemed too easy. He sarcastically called the doctrine "easy grace" because he felt it let people off the hook who *deserved* to be punished.

After several years of friendship, I discovered that this man was hiding a great secret, a terrible sin in his past for which he could not forgive himself. In his mind this sin was so horrible that justice must surely bar him from the kingdom of God forever. He was absolutely without hope, and in his stony resignation to what he considered a just fate, he had become hard and cold and dead. His self-hatred and rage at his own imperfection spiraled outward to wound everyone he knew who might also show signs of imperfection.

As we talked it over on one occasion, I agreed that he was probably right about the law of justice—it probably would slam the door of the kingdom in his face. But I also reminded him that mercy could open doors justice wouldn't. Then I took a gamble and told him that I didn't think his fixation for justice was motivated by grief and guilt, as he claimed, but rather by pride. He just couldn't tolerate the thought that he was as other men. He couldn't tolerate the thought that he needed help, nor could he lower himself to ask for it. He was willing to accept the fact that others were spiritually inept, but that *he* couldn't save himself, that *he* needed someone else's help—that was just too monstrous, too grotesque to consider. His pride would not allow it. So he rejected mercy, even though he couldn't satisfy justice. Consequently, his heart had not broken under its weight of sin—it just turned to stone instead. He would rather be damned by justice than ask God for mercy.

At first he was offended by what I said, and for a while our friendship hung in the balance. But little by little he realized that his rejection of the idea of mercy amounted to a rejection of Christ. Finally one day he said, "That's really it, isn't it. I'm just too proud to admit my weakness and ask for help. I don't want to admit my imperfection even to myself, let alone to the bishop or to God. My pride would rather see me in hell paying the full penalty of justice than see me humble myself to seek the Lord's mercy." Eventually he went to his bishop and with considerable courage confessed a sin carefully hidden for decades. And as he humbled himself and sought mercy rather than justice for himself in his own life, a marvelous thing happened. As he came to know he was forgiven by grace for someone else's sake, as he realized what had been done for him as a favor, as he realized what an incredible break he had been given *gratis*, he began to act with patience and mercy and forgiveness toward those around him. He was no longer a hard man.

But why would You do this for me?

Because I love you.

But it doesn't seem fair.

That's right. It's not fair at all—it's merciful.

It is, after all, a gift.

But how can I possibly deserve such a gift?

82

Don't be silly. You can't. You don't. This gift
is offered because I love you and want to
help you, not because I owe it to you.
But how can I ever repay You?
There you go again. Don't you get it yet?
You *can't* repay me, not you or all the billions
like you. Gifts of this magnitude can never
be repaid. For what I've done out of love for you,
you can only love me back, and seek to become
what I am—a giver of good gifts.

And that is good news.

Chapter Five

MISUNDERSTANDING GRACE

The doctrine of grace is susceptible to misunderstanding or distortion in several ways. Perhaps the most serious distortion is to argue that since in the covenant relationship Christ makes up what I lack, I don't need to work as hard anymore. I can relax and let Jesus do everything for me; I can just coast along with a token effort, clinging tenaciously to my favorite sins, and still expect to be "saved by grace."

In the early Christian Church, the Apostle Paul was confronted by those who thought grace would be a license and a shield for sin: "What then? shall we sin, because we are not under the law, but under grace? God forbid. Know ye not, that to whom ye yield yourselves servants to obey, his servants ye are to whom ye obey; whether of sin unto death, or of obedience unto righteousness." (Rom. 6:15–16.)

The false doctrine of salvation by grace without commitment or loyalty violates the terms of the gospel covenant by asking Jesus to do for me what I could very well do for myself — but don't *want* to. Anyone can *pretend* to be doing their best and *pretend* to be justified by faith in Christ and to enjoy the companionship of the Holy Ghost, while in truth they remain obstinately committed to their sins. No one but God knows they are lying. I wish I could offer an objective test for distinguishing between the honest in heart who strive to do what they can and the pretenders who expect to be carried when they could walk, but I don't know how to do it. I am content that God knows the difference.

Certainly those who say, "I'm doing the best I can," but then willfully break the commandments need to learn the difference between *wanting* righteousness and *wishing* they wanted righteousness. Though God may accept righteous intentions and desires in place of perfect performance, he takes no wooden nickels. He will not accept in place of righteous intentions and desires mere *wishes* that we had some. The latter is not a commitment. It is not faithful. It does not meet the obligations of the gospel covenant — and it receives no promise. For in these cases the individuals don't really hunger and thirst after righteousness but after sin, and they expect Jesus to tolerate it or even to subsidize it. These have broken their covenant. Doctrine and Covenants 50:7–8 says, "Verily I say unto you, there are hypocrites among you, who have deceived some. . . . But the hypocrites shall be detected and shall be cut off, either in life or in death, even as I will."

Individuals who commit the moral and doctrinal error of refusing to do what they could very well do seek to be saved *in* their sins rather than *from* their sins. But that can never happen. There is a vast difference between viewing my sins as enemies from which I'm trying with difficulty to escape and viewing my sins as comfortable old friends I'm reluctant to leave behind. There is a difference between being unable to conquer all my sins right now, in which case the covenant promises me hope, and being unwilling even to try, in which case I am left to face justice alone. The covenant offers grace and forgiveness through ongoing repentance both to those who try and succeed and to those who try but fail yet try again. However, there is no forgiveness for those who will not try, or who try once or twice without success and then give up.

"EASY" GRACE

On one occasion I was lecturing on a related subject in a small town in Nevada. I explained that perfection was not required of us all at once but that we are obligated to do all we can while the Savior has promised to do the rest. After the lecture someone came up to me and said, "Dr. Robinson, do you know what this means? It means I don't have to can peaches this year!" At this there was a general round of laughter, but when it subsided, I quickly responded, "Oh no, my friend, you have misunderstood me. That's not what it means at all. If you really believe that God expects you to can peaches (and that's an arguable proposition), then you must can all the peaches you're *able* to can. All this doctrine means is that you don't need to feel guilty or worry about the peaches you *can't* can."

This is not a doctrine of "easy" grace. There is no virtue one might have possessed before entering the covenant that one may then discard or renounce upon entering the covenant — without violating the covenant. The gospel covenant is not an excuse to work beneath our abilities. The covenant requires more than merely *wishing* we were better; we've got to actually *do* what is within our power. Although personal perfection is not required of us right now, our best attempt at it is. The good news is that God will not require of us more than the best we can do, but the bad news is he will not accept less than that either.

Moreover, there is really no such thing as "easy" grace because the partnership with Christ isn't easy — it calls for the best and the highest within us. He requires our loyalty, our service to God with all our heart, might, mind, and strength. He demands ongoing repentance and continual recommitment. And he offers no proof and no guarantee beyond the private witness of the Spirit that he can do what he promises. Rather, he asks us to trust him, to accept his word on faith.

The Lord's present law of temporal salvation (the welfare program) works on essentially the same terms as its spiritual counterpart. Individuals in need of temporal help are required to contribute all they can toward the desired goal. They are required to expend all their own resources, however great or small these may be. Then the Lord through the Church and its members adds whatever else may be necessary. When properly administered, the temporal arrangement is a partnership that meets an individual's honest needs while still demanding his or her best efforts. Moreover, the arrangement assumes progress will be made, and it aims eventually at making the individual self-sufficient.

The principle of spiritual welfare is no different. As we demonstrate our good faith by doing all that we can and consecrating all our own resources to the common purpose, the grace of God and the atonement of Christ are sufficient to meet all our other needs, but the covenant still demands our best efforts, assumes progress will be made, and aims at eventually making us self-sufficient as far as righteousness is concerned.

GOSPEL SUPERLATIVES

A second common distortion of the doctrine of grace, less sinister perhaps than "easy" grace but I think more widespread in the Church, is the view that the Savior extends his grace to us only *after* we've done all we possibly can do. It would follow then that since no one ever really does *all* they possibly, theoretically could have done, no one can ever really be worthy of grace either. The false logic runs like this:

> 1. Grace and mercy are given only to those who are worthy of it, and only *after* they have proved they are worthy.
> 2. Only those who keep all the commandments of God all the time are really worthy.
> 3. But I can't keep all the commandments all the time.
> 4. Therefore, I'm not really worthy and can never expect to receive grace and mercy.

This kind of thinking is merely the old demand for total perfection trying to sneak in the back door of the Church in a gospel disguise, and it mocks the atonement of Christ by insisting that we must perfect and save ourselves before the Savior can save us, that we must first cure ourselves before we deserve to call a doctor. Such logic would make it impossible for Christ to save anyone, ever. Unfortunately, sometimes even the scripturally literate will limit their concept of grace in this way without realizing that, in the long run, it turns the doctrine of grace into salvation by works. Just as mercy isn't mercy if we deserve it, so grace isn't grace if we earn it.

There are a great many superlatives used in the scriptures and the Church to exhort the Saints and describe their obligations: *all* our heart, our *greatest* desire, our *best* effort, after *all* we can do, *always*, *every*, *never*, and so on. We must remember that applied to mortals these terms are aspirational — that is, they define our desires and set our goals — that in each case the circumstances of the individual determine what "all," "the best," or "the greatest" mean, and that "never," "every," or "always" are goals to be reached with the help of Christ and through his atonement.

"AFTER ALL WE CAN DO"

In my opinion some of the blame for our misapplication of gospel superlatives and other similarly obsessive reasoning comes from a misunderstanding of 2 Nephi 25:23: "For we labor diligently to write, to persuade our children, and also our brethren, to believe in Christ, and to be reconciled to God; for we know that it is by grace that we are saved, *after* all we can do." (Italics added.)

At first glance at this scripture, we might think that grace is offered to us only chronologically after we have completed doing all we can do, but this is demonstrably false, for we have already received many manifestations of God's grace before we even come to this point. By his grace, we live and breathe. By grace, we are spiritually begotten children of heavenly parents and enjoy divine prospects. By grace, a plan was prepared and a savior designated for humanity when Adam and Eve fell. By grace, the good news of this gospel comes to us and informs us of our eternal options. By grace, we have the agency to accept the gospel when we hear it. By the grace that comes through faith in Christ, we start the repentance process; and by grace, we are justified and made part of God's kingdom even while that process is still incomplete. The grace of God has been involved in our spiritual progress from the beginning and will be involved in our progress until the end.

It therefore belittles God's grace to think of it as only a cherry on top added at the last moment as a mere finishing touch to what we have already accomplished on our own without any help from God. Instead the reverse would be a truer proposition: our efforts are the cherry on top added to all that God has already done for us.

Actually, I understand the preposition "after" in 2 Nephi 25:23 to be a preposition of separation rather than a preposition of time. It denotes logical separateness rather than temporal sequence. We are saved by grace "apart from all we can do," or "all we can do notwithstanding," or even "regardless of all we can do." Another acceptable paraphrase of the sense of the verse might read, "We are still saved by grace, after all is said and done."

In addition, even the phrase "all we can do" is susceptible to a sinister interpretation as meaning every single good deed we could conceivably have ever done. This is nonsense. If grace could operate only in such cases, no one could ever be saved, not even the best among us. It is precisely because we *don't* always do everything we could have done that we need a savior in the first place, so obviously we can't make doing everything we could have done a condition for receiving grace and being saved! I believe the emphasis in 2 Nephi 25:23 is meant to fall on the word *we* ("all *we* can do," as opposed to all *he* can do). Moreover, "all we can do" here should probably be understood in the sense of "everything we can do," or even "whatever we can do."

Thus, the correct sense of 2 Nephi 25:23 would be that we are ultimately saved by grace apart from whatever we manage to do. Grace is not merely a decorative touch or a finishing bit of trim to top off our own efforts—it is God's participation in the process of our salvation from its beginning to its end. Though I must be intimately involved in the process of my salvation, in the long run the success of that venture is utterly dependent upon the grace of Christ.

BUT WHEN HAVE I DONE ENOUGH?

I have a friend who always asks at about this point, "But when have I done enough? How can I know that I've made it?" This misunderstands the doctrine of grace by asking the wrong question. The right question is "When is my offering *acceptable* to the Lord? When are my efforts accepted *for the time being*?" You see, the answer to the former question, "When have I done enough?" is *never* in this life. Since the goal is perfection, the Lord can never unconditionally approve an imperfect performance. No matter how much we do in mortality, no matter how well we perform, the demand to do better, the pressure to improve and to make progress, will never go away. We have not yet arrived.

In this life we are all unprofitable servants, or to use a more modern term, we are all bad investments. (See, for example, Luke 17:10; Mosiah 2:21.) From the Savior's perspective, even the most righteous among us cost more to save and maintain than we can produce in return. So if we're looking for the Lord to say, "OK, you've done enough. Your obligation is fulfilled. You've made it, now relax," we're going to be disappointed. We need to accept the fact that we will never in this life, even through our most valiant efforts, reach the break-even point. We are all unprofitable servants being carried along on the Savior's back by his good will—by his grace.

However, the Lord does say to us, "Given your present circumstances and your present level of maturity, you're doing a decent job. Of course it's not perfect, but your efforts are acceptable for the time being. I am pleased with what you've done." We may not be profitable servants yet in the ultimate sense, but we can still be good and faithful ones in this limited sense. So if we are doing what can reasonably be expected of a loyal disciple in our present circumstances, then we can have faith that our offering is accepted through the grace of God. Of course we're unprofitable—all of us. Yet within the shelter of the covenant, our honest attempts are acceptable for the time being.

In fact, there is a way we can know that our efforts are acceptable, that our covenant is recognized and valid before God. If we experience the gifts of the Spirit or the influence of the Holy Ghost, we can know that we are in the covenant relationship, for the gifts and companionship of the Holy Ghost are given to none else. This is one reason why the gift of the Holy Ghost is given—as a token and assurance of our covenant status and as a down payment to us on the blessings and glory to come if we are faithful. Paul refers to the Holy Ghost as "the earnest of our inheritance" (Eph. 1:14), a reference to "earnest money," which, though only a token payment, makes a deal binding when it changes hands. Thus the "earnest [money] of the Spirit in our hearts" (2 Cor. 1:22; 5:5) assures us of the validity and efficacy of our deal, our covenant, with God.

Do you feel the influence of the Holy Ghost in your life? Do you enjoy the gifts of the Spirit? Then you can *know* that God accepts your faith, repentance, and baptism and has agreed that "[you] may always have his Spirit to be with [you]." (D&C 20:77.) This is perhaps one reason why the Holy Ghost is called the Comforter, because if we enjoy that gift, we can know that our efforts are acceptable—for now – and that we are justified before God by our faith in Christ. And that is comfort indeed.

GIVING HIM EVERYTHING

So what does it mean to give him everything? Some of us simply have more ability, more talents, than others. Yet according to the parable, those with only one talent or only two talents are not expected to earn five. Only the one with five talents is expected to earn five.

Let me illustrate with an example. Many years ago I came into contact with a woman who was, initially at least, one of the roughest persons I have ever known. Abused as a child, she had run away from home and had lived on the streets for years. As a young woman, she traveled around the country with a motorcycle gang. In late middle age, her beauty gone, she spent most of her time in a pub, where some missionaries met her when they went in to get change for a pay phone outside. When she was baptized, many of the members worried that her conversion wouldn't last, and there were good reasons to suspect it might not.

For a long time after her baptism, this sister still swore like a trooper, even in Church, and never quite lived the Word of Wisdom one hundred percent. On one occasion during her first year in the Church, she lost her temper during a Relief Society meeting and punched out one of the other sisters. Her ex-husband is an alcoholic, and her children have all spent time in jail.

Now the question before us is whether someone like this can seriously expect to be saved. What hope does a person like this, with all her faults and weaknesses, really have? With her background and problems, why bother coming to Church at all?

"Though your sins be as scarlet, they shall be as white as snow; though they be red like crimson, they shall be as wool." God does not lie. Whoever will come, may come. All are invited; none is excluded. Though this sister had further to travel than most, the same covenant was offered to her: "Do all you can. I will do the rest while you learn how." And she was as faithful as she could be under her circumstances. She never said, "No, I won't," or "Get off my back," or "Why talk to me? Talk to him, he started it." She always said, "I know; I'm sorry. I'll try to do better." Then she would try to do better. Often she would fail, but little by little over the years, she improved a great deal. First she gave up coffee, tea, and alcohol. Then she stopped swearing. Later she overcame smoking and got her temper somewhat under control. Finally, after she'd been in the Church many years, she was ready to go to the temple. Can such a person really expect to inherit the kingdom of God? Of course.

But now the harder question. At what point did this sister become a candidate for the kingdom? Was it when she finally gave up cigarettes, or when she got her language and temper under control? Or was it when she finally qualified for a temple recommend? No. It was none of these, though they were all important landmarks in her progress. She was justified through her faith in Jesus Christ on the day that she repented of her sins, was baptized, and received the gift of the Holy Ghost, for she entered into that covenant in good faith and in all sincerity. She believed in Christ, and she believed Christ. Like the widow with her mite, she gave all she had and held nothing back. It may not have been much, but it was everything.

Every week she took the sacrament, having repented of her mistakes and resolving again to eliminate them. Some things took years to overcome. Other things perhaps haven't been overcome yet, but she still tries, and she won't give up. And as long as she won't give up but endures to the end in the gospel harness, pulling toward the kingdom, her reward is sure. God knows our circumstances, and he judges us accordingly. He knows who is standing in a hole and who is standing on a chair, and he does not just measure height—he measures growth.

Each of us operates at a different level of performance within the covenant boundaries. The percentages vary both from person to person and, even for the same person, over a period of time. In my case, my efforts might take me twenty percent of the way to perfection. The Savior covers the other eighty percent. In your case, your efforts might take you fifty percent—or two percent—of the way. The Savior *still* covers the difference. But in every case the sum of the joint effort is the same—anyone's best efforts, however great or small, plus the atonement of Christ will equal 100 percent of what is needed to enter God's kingdom.

FALSE PERFECTION

Then what does it mean to be perfect? And why are we commanded in the scriptures to be perfect? (See Matt. 5:48;

3 Ne. 12:48.) Actually, I dislike the word *perfect* because it is often misused. I frequently wince when I hear it in talks or lessons, because more often than not it is used with its philosophical meaning of "unimprovable," and this is almost *never* its scriptural meaning. Latter-day Saints believe in *eternal* progress. No one can ever be "unimprovable" in the ultimate sense. Rather, to be perfect in this life is to enter into the covenant of the gospel and receive perfection-in-Christ.[1]

So far in this book I have myself used the word *perfect* to mean without error, fault, or blemish, but even this is different from the usual scriptural sense. In the New Testament the Greek word translated "perfect" is *teleios*. It means ripe, mature, ready, complete, whole, and so forth. An apple on the tree might be called *teleios* when it was ripe and ready to be picked, but that doesn't mean it was an unimprovable apple. It might still have a worm in it.

Here is another of the great secrets: To be perfect means to be doing the best you can do under the circumstances you are in. As Brigham Young once explained:

> We all occupy diversified stations in the world, and the kingdom of God. Those who do right, and seek the glory of the Father in heaven, whether their knowledge be little or much, or whether they can do little, or much, if they do the very best they know how, *they are perfect.* . . . "Be ye as perfect as ye can," for that is all we can do, though it is written, "Be ye perfect

---

[1]See chapter 2, pp. 13–14, 23–30.

as your Father who is in heaven is perfect." To be as perfect as we possibly can, according to our knowledge, is to be just as perfect as our Father in heaven is. He cannot be any more perfect than He knows how, any more than we. When we are doing as well as we know how in the sphere and station which we occupy here, we are justified.[2]

Brigham Young can say that doing the best we know how is being perfect because it fulfills our part of the covenant, and as we do this, Jesus Christ fulfills his part of the covenant and makes us perfect through his merit and mercy. The perfection we receive in this manner is perfection-in-Christ. This is also the perfection that allows us to enter the celestial kingdom. The other perfection, the actual, personal, "I-never-make-a-mistake" kind of perfection comes even later than that—much later.

It is reported that someone once challenged the work of Mother Theresa, the holy woman who ministers to the poorest outcasts in Calcutta, India, on the grounds that she could never succeed at what she was trying to do. No matter how hard she worked, her antagonist insisted, there would be more of the poor and sick tomorrow than there were today, and all her efforts could never even make a dent in the problem. Since she could never hope to succeed, why did she waste her efforts in a losing cause? Mother Theresa's answer was a classic. "God does not require that I succeed," she replied, "only that I do what I can." And that is the gospel truth.

---

[2]*Journal of Discourses,* 2:129–30; italics added.

THEN WHY THE DEMAND FOR MORE?

Unfortunately, people are frequently asked in the Church to do more than they really can do. I remember one Sunday in priesthood meeting in Durham, North Carolina, when the elders were asked to donate just one Saturday that month to each of six worthy but separate projects. Now this occurred in a month with only four Saturdays in it. In short, filling all six assignments was not physically possible for anyone, but when this was pointed out, none of the obligations were repealed. Each individual was just left to do "the best he could."

Several years ago, as I read Matthew 11:28–30, about Jesus' yoke being easy and his burden being light, to a New Testament class, a female student at the back of the class interrupted me with a loud "Ha!" When I invited her to explain what she meant by her outburst, she said, "His yoke is easy? His burden is light? Anyone in this church who believes that is either a recent convert or brain-dead."

This sister was a divorced mother of several children who was back in school trying to get a better life for herself and her family. She continued: "I used to try to do and be everything that the Church wanted, but I finally had to give up. They always wanted more than I had. I can't help that I'm broke or that I'm a single parent with two jobs trying to go to school full-time. I can't do what the other Saints can, and they always want more out of me – more time, more talent, more money, more commitment – and I just don't have more to give. The demands of the Church exceed my supply."

Why does the Church sometimes seem to demand more of me than I think I can do? Why is there always so much pressure for me to be and to do and to give *more*? Well, first of all we've got to remember that perfection is the goal, a real goal, and we should be working for it with all our best efforts. We just need to remember at the same time that our salvation is *not* hanging in the balance.

For example, when I was in high school, I used to work out in the weight room. In those days of free weights, a spotter always stood next to the bench to grab the bar when I got in trouble. But invariably there was a little ritual exchange, familiar to all who have worked out in a gym, that went like this. After doing all the repetitions with the barbell that I was able to, being on the brink of collapse, I would say to the spotter, "Take it!" But the spotter would always say, "No, do one more!" Usually by reaching way down deep, I could in fact manage one more rep, after which I would say, "OK, take it!" Again the spotter would reply, "No, do one more." Now understand that no matter how many times I did "just one more" by whatever superhuman effort, when that one was done, the spotter would *still* say, "Just one more!" This would continue until my muscles actually gave out, and then the spotter would grab the bar.

Now when this would happen, I was not so naïve as to say, "I'm humiliated, embarrassed, and offended. You wanted one more rep, and I couldn't do it. You ask too much of me; you always want more than I can give. I can't cope with your demands. I'm going home, and I'm never coming back." I didn't feel this way because in a gym both the spotters and the lifters understand that the real power is gained on the last repetition, on the thin edge between what one can do and what one can't. By coaxing me into working at the limits of my abilities, the spotter helped me develop the power I was seeking. There was never embarrassment that I couldn't do that last rep, and no one seriously expected it, but I did get the satisfaction of knowing that I had worked out to the limits of my strength and that it was making me stronger.

I believe the same principle can be applied to the seemingly heavy demands of the Church. One purpose of the Church is to perfect the Saints. Since we make the most progress by working at the limits of our abilities, then no matter how much we do or how well we do it, the Lord—like the spotter in the gym—will always ask for more, will always seek improvement, will always push us toward perfection. Since our very real goal is perfection, the demands of the Spotter can be turned up to infinity and will exceed the abilities of any individual. We just need to remember that our salvation is not hanging in the balance, for that issue is already settled if we are keeping our covenants. We shouldn't get embarrassed when we reach our limits or take offense when we can't do all that is asked of us. Rather, we must learn to take satisfaction in performing at the limits of our ability (for that is where the real power is gained) and let God worry about the rest. When pressed by the demands of perfection, we must remind ourselves that our best efforts will be accepted as payment in full—at least for now.

The "easiness" of the Savior's yoke does not mean we

can expect to be excused from the hard tasks of life or be immune to its hard realities. (Ask Job or the Mormon pioneers about that.) Rather his yoke is easy (a) because it makes what was formerly impossible possible and (b) because he grants compensatory blessings and grace to help us through the hard times. The yoke of the law of Moses could not even be lifted, but the yoke of Christ can be lifted and carried because its weight is individually adapted to our abilities and strength. In this sense "easy" does not mean "totally without effort," rather it means "totally within our power." But even beyond this, those who assume his yoke in humble obedience and consecrate their efforts to him soon learn that an unseen hand lightens the load in the rough spots and leaves blessings out of all proportion to the required sacrifices.

INDIVIDUAL PERFECTION

But will I ever be perfect in the sense of being without error, fault, or blemish? I mean me separately and individually, apart from my covenant perfection-in-Christ? I think the answer is yes. For example, I envision a scene about a million years from now, after we've been in the celestial kingdom a very, very long time. I will approach the Savior and say something like, "OK, I finally did it. I have overcome eating fruit out of season (or whatever). Now what comes next?" And he will look at me and say, "Hey—that was it! Congratulations! That was the last one. You have finally learned to keep all the commandments all of the time!"

And I suppose we'll invite in the neighborhood and have a little "Steve-finally-made-it" party.

But that's a million years from now, and long after the resurrection of the just. In the meantime, my only hope is that Christ will carry me on his shoulders. Between now and then, my only hope of perfection is the perfection-in-Christ that he shares with those in the gospel covenant, for that very perfection-in-Christ and nothing else is what will allow me into the celestial kingdom at the day of judgment.

THE COMFORT OF KNOWING

Many years ago Janet and I had a friend who did not understand how grace worked and who would frequently say something like this: "Well, I figure my life is about half over, and I'm about halfway to the celestial kingdom, so I'm right on schedule." One day I asked her, "Judy, what would happen if you died tomorrow, where would you end up in eternity?" Apparently the thought had never occurred to her. She thought for a moment, then said, "Well, let's see, halfway to the celestial kingdom is . . . midterrestrial! That's not good enough, is it?"

No, it's not good enough. It's also not the gospel. We need to know that in this covenant relationship we have with the Savior, if we should die tomorrow, we have hope of the celestial kingdom. And that hope is one of the promised blessings of the covenant relationship: "Let us cheerfully do all things that lie in our power; and then may we stand still, *with the utmost assurance,* to see the salvation of God, and for his arm to be revealed." (D&C 123:17;

italics added. See also D&C 106:8; Eph. 3:12.) When we have done what lies in our power, we may have and should have the "utmost assurance" of the salvation of God. Part of the comfort given by the Holy Ghost is knowing that even though I am imperfect, if I die in the covenant, I will still inherit the kingdom of God. In fact, since *everyone* dies while he or she is still imperfect, it couldn't be any other way.

Some of the best news of all is that Christ *promises* us that our mistakes will not be held against us if we will just maintain the covenant relationship throughout our lives. He who cannot lie *promises* that we will receive the kingdom of God: "Whoso repenteth and is baptized in my name shall be filled; and if he endureth to the end, behold, him will I hold guiltless before my Father at that day when I shall stand to judge the world." (3 Ne. 27:16.) Nephi vouches for this too. He heard the Father's voice saying, "Yea, the words of my Beloved are true and faithful. He that endureth to the end, the same shall be saved." (2 Ne. 31:15.)

Can the Father and the Son lie? Of course not. Then if we have faith in Christ and repent of our sins, if we are baptized and receive the gift of the Holy Ghost, if we remain willing and keep our covenants, then how can we doubt that we shall, through the atonement of Christ, inherit the kingdom of God? With such promises as these, who dares to doubt the truth of it?

When the prophet Enos heard the voice of Christ tell him, "Thy sins are forgiven thee, and thou shalt be blessed," he responded, "I, Enos knew that God could not lie; wherefore, my guilt was swept away." (Enos 1:5–6.) Often those who wrestle with spiritual things want to "feel" the results before they will believe that anything has happened. This is backward. They want to feel a confirmation, the blessings of belief, *before* they will believe. Notice that Enos did not subjectively "feel" his guilt leave and then believe. Quite the opposite. He knew his guilt was gone because Christ told him it was gone, and he believed Christ.

Moreover, "enduring to the end" does not mean "enduring in perfection." Rather it means enduring in the covenant of faith and repentance. Thus we see that faith in Christ, repentance, and the cleansing of the Atonement cannot be one-time events in our lives. Although they may begin on a particular occasion, faith, repentance, and forgiveness are part of a continual process of rejecting our mistakes, reaffirming our desires and our goal, and realigning our lives to Christ whenever and wherever we are off track.

TRUST ME

When our twin daughters were small, Janet and I took the family to a public swimming pool for family home evening. Our intention was to teach the girls how to swim. After we got situated, I picked up Rebekah and started walking into the shallow end of the pool. As we walked into the water, I was thinking, "Gee, what a swell dad I am. This is a great family home evening." But as she felt the water rising around her, her thoughts were, "My dad is going to drown me. I'm going to die." Now the water was only three-and-a-half feet deep, but Rebekah was only three feet deep.

She was so terrified of what was, in her mind, deep water, that she started to kick and scratch and scream. In her panic, she was absolutely unteachable.

Finally, I had to grab her and wrap my arms around her, then just hold her and say, "Becky, calm down! I'm your dad, and I love you. I'm not going to let anything happen to you. You're perfectly safe. Now relax and *trust* me!" And bless her heart, she stopped fighting, she relaxed, and she trusted me. Then, and only then, could I put my hands under her and hold her out of the water. I said, "Okay, now kick your legs. Very good. Now kick harder." And so she began to learn how to swim.

This is very much like what is happening to some of us in our spiritual lives. Some of us are so paralyzed by fear of our sins that we can't learn how to overcome them. Sometimes we're so worried about whether we're going to live or die, or whether we've made it to the kingdom, that we cannot make any real spiritual progress. Our lack of faith in Christ makes us worry about our spiritual status and doubt God's promises. I know people who agonize daily, "Was I good enough today? Did my righteous deeds outweigh my sins? Did I make the cut-off? Am I in the kingdom, or not?" As in Becky's experience with swimming, their fear gets in the way of learning and progressing. Spiritual panic cripples them.

At times like this, when the rising panic begins to paralyze us, we must believe Christ. We must hear his voice, "Stephen, calm down! I'm your Father, and I love you. I'm not going to let anything happen to you. I've got you! You're perfectly safe. Now relax and *trust* me, and I'll teach you what you need to do." Then he supports us in his arms and says, "OK, now pay your tithing. Pretty good. Now pay a *full* tithing." And so we begin to learn perfection. "Thus mercy can satisfy the demands of justice, and encircles them in the arms of safety." (Alma 34:16.) "In the arms of safety" — my favorite phrase from the Book of Mormon. In the gospel covenant, we are encircled in the arms of safety — His arms. "You're OK. You're going to make it. *Trust* me."

And that is good news.

Chapter Six

"LORD, HOW IS IT DONE?"[1]

Up to now we have looked at the Atonement from the perspective of those who are benefited by it. We have examined the practical issues of what the Atonement means for us and how our lives can be changed. Now we must look at the Atonement from the perspective of the One who atones, of the Savior rather than of the saved. How is it that Christ can draw upon this vast ocean of merit and mercy in my behalf? What gives him the power to save? Exactly who was he, what did he do for me, why did he do it, and what did it cost him?

THE DIVINITY OF CHRIST

First of all, Jesus was God, not only the Son of God or the Elder Brother, but *God* in his own right. Before he became flesh and blood, he was known and worshiped as Jehovah;

---

[1]Enos 1:7.

109

the Lord God Almighty; the God of Abraham, Isaac, and Jacob; the God of Israel. The Apostle Paul explains that Jesus Christ is the creator of all things and that he is the power that holds all things together in their created state: "For by him were all things created, that are in heaven, and that are in earth, visible and invisible, whether they be thrones, or dominions, or principalities, or powers: all things were created by him, and for him: and he is before all things, and by him all things consist." (Col. 1:16.) The Apostle John says much the same thing, though emphasizing that Jesus Christ is the source of life and light: "All things were made by him, and without him was not any thing made that was made. In him was life; and the life was the light of men." (John 1:3–4.)

The Book of Mormon prophets further testify of the divinity of Jesus Christ. For example, Nephi declares: "The God of our fathers, who were led out of Egypt, out of bondage, and also were preserved in the wilderness by him, yea, the God of Abraham, and of Isaac, and the God of Jacob, yieldeth himself, according to the words of the angel, as a man, into the hands of wicked men, to be lifted up, according to the words of Zenock, and to be crucified, according to the words of Neum, and to be buried in a sepulchre, according to the words of Zenos." (1 Ne. 19:10.)

During the events associated with the Atonement, God — in the person of God the Son, Jesus Christ — took moral responsibility for all the negatives — the suffering, pain, and death — that are a necessary part of the plan of God. This plan, defended and championed by Jesus before the world was, asks us to live in an imperfect, fallen world. At times it asks us to suffer; it asks some of us to suffer horribly. It is therefore only fair that the God who administers such a plan and who asks us to live by it should himself be willing to suffer under its provisions more than any of us. And this he did in the events of Gethsemane and Calvary. There Jesus Christ confirmed his right to ask us to suffer for him by his willingness to suffer, bleed, and die for us. In the gospel of Jesus Christ, there are no "fall guys." Nobody gets stuck with the short end of the stick for what God proposes, for he who proposed the plan is the one who suffers the most under it. This gives him the moral right to say, "It is a good plan; it's the right thing."

Occasionally some critics have suggested that Christianity is just another religion of human sacrifice. There might be something to the claim if Jesus Christ were not God, if he were only another human being. After all, if the Atonement is merely a case of God demanding the blood of a human victim in order to be reconciled to humanity and forgive us, how is this any different in principle from grabbing some poor virgin and throwing her into a volcano to save the village, or from burning children on an altar to Moloch to win his good favor? The profound difference is that in these latter cases the intent is that human beings suffer to reconcile God to humanity, while in Christianity God himself—Jesus Christ—suffers and dies to reconcile humanity to himself and to his Father. We're not trying to reach God and touch his heart with *our* sacrifices, rather God is trying to reach us and touch our hearts with *his* infinite sacrifice. The sacrificial Lamb of God who died on Calvary was God.

THE HUMANITY OF CHRIST

But according to the scriptures, Jesus was not only divine, he was also fully and genuinely human: "The Word was made flesh, and dwelt among us, (and we beheld his glory, the glory as of the only begotten of the Father,) full of grace and truth." (John 1:14.) "Wherefore *in all things* it behooved him to be made like unto his brethren, that he might be a merciful and faithful high priest in things pertaining to God, to make reconciliation for the sins of the people. For in that *he himself hath suffered being tempted*, he is able to succour them that are tempted." (Heb. 2:17–18; italics added.)

A remarkable doctrine is taught here. The same Jesus Christ who is God the Son is also one of us. He was human in every respect ("in all things") — right down to being tempted like other human beings. And because he personally has been tempted, Christ can understand what temptation is. From his own personal experience of the human condition, he understands what we are dealing with here, and he can empathize with us and help us overcome temptation just as he overcame it.

But can Jesus Christ, the divine son of God, *really* have been tempted? Let me put the question more pointedly: Did Jesus Christ have a carnal nature and suffer carnal urges? Did he ever feel his flesh say "yes!" and have to say "no!"

to it? Did he ever experience the *enticement*, the carnal appeal, of sin?

Many Christians want to answer, "No, Christ was too holy to experience real temptations," but I believe the correct answer, the scriptural answer, is yes. Jesus was human like the rest of us. Part of what the Book of Mormon calls the great condescension of God was Christ's willingness to come into a mortal body that would subject him to physical temptations. (See 1 Ne. 11:13–32.) Jesus' holiness and perfect obedience were the result of consistently ignoring, rather than of never encountering, the enticements of a carnal nature. The righteousness of Jesus is that he experienced the same temptations, the same carnal urges, the same distractions and opposition of the flesh and of the mind that we do in mortality, yet he instantly rejected them in every case: "He suffered temptations but gave no heed unto them." (D&C 20:22.)

Think about it. If Christ were not like us in being subject to temptation, if he were some different kind of being with qualitatively different experiences, how could he possibly set an example that we could follow? How could his person or his performance then be relevant to *human* beings? It doesn't matter how patiently a bird might show me how to fly, or a fish might show me how to breathe underwater. I don't have wings, and I don't have gills. These cannot teach me by example because we are not the same kind of being. Similarly, if Jesus Christ was not genuinely human, or if his righteousness and obedience were due to some special gift that I do not share with him, then he cannot teach me by example to be like he is.

In ancient times there was a heresy known as *docetism*, which taught that Jesus wasn't really human, that he only appeared or *seemed* to be human.[2] Influenced by hellenistic thinking, docetists insisted that being human was utterly incompatible with being divine. Feeling it necessary to choose between Jesus' humanity and his divinity, they concluded that Jesus was divine and not human; despite the witness of the scriptures, they declared that his humanity was merely an illusion.

Whenever someone proposes that Jesus' experience in mortality was different in kind from that common to the rest of humanity, or that his righteousness and perfection were based on factors unavailable to the rest of us, this is, to a degree, a modern form of docetism. The mortal Jesus Christ was the *best* of us — but he was *one* of us, and being tempted is part of being human. His flesh was human flesh, and his experience was human experience. Hence the author of Hebrews insists that "[Christ] himself hath suffered being tempted." (2:18.)

Moreover, being tempted, even being tempted greatly or over a long period of time, is not in itself a sin. We seldom choose what we will be tempted by, or how strong or how frequent our temptations will be. Still, as long as we resist them, we remain innocent. Thus, for the scripture to main-

---

[2]The term *docetism* comes from the Greek verb *dokeo*, which means "to seem" or "to appear."

tain that he "hath suffered being tempted" does not insult the Savior or detract from his moral perfection.

Do not misunderstand me. I am not suggesting here that Jesus in any way indulged in unclean thoughts, for that would be sin, and he indulged nothing sinful. I do not believe that he "struggled" or "wrestled" with temptations. My only point is that he was as vulnerable to suggestions and impulses coming into his mind from his mortal nature, a nature inherited from his mortal mother, as any of us. He simply paid no attention to those suggestions, and he immediately put them out of his mind. The ability of the flesh to suggest, to entice, was the same for him as it is for us, but unlike the rest of us, he *never* responded to it. He didn't ponder, deliberate, or entertain the sinful options even as theoretical possibilities—"he gave no heed unto them."

"We have not an high priest which cannot be touched with the feeling of our infirmities; but was *in all points tempted like as we are*, yet without sin." (Heb. 4:15; italics added.) Because he "was in all points tempted like as we are," our Savior understands our situation, knows from his own personal experience what we struggle against, and can sympathize with us and have compassion on us. Thus, when I am tempted, I don't have to appeal to some distant entity who has never been in my shoes. I can take my problems to a high priest, Jesus, who *can* "be touched with the feeling of my infirmities"—because he has been where I am. I can share my problems with a compassionate God who knows from experience what I am talking about and understands from experience what I am going through. There may be certain aspects of his nature that the rest of us do not fully share, but there is no aspect of our human nature that he does not share. And that is good news.

VICARIOUS SUFFERING

Still, some are haunted by the final three words in Hebrews 4:15, "yet without sin." After all, human beings aren't just *tempted* to sin — they actually *do* it. Since I have on occasion given in to my temptations and Jesus never did, since I am guilty and he never was, how can he understand the sinner? How can our Savior claim to be fully human and to understand human beings if he has never experienced human sin and guilt? How can a perfect, sinless being comprehend my private agony of unworthiness? Does he know what it's like to look in a mirror and despise what he sees looking back at him? Does he know what it is to wander through the ashes of a life destroyed by one's own choices? Human beings are inevitably the arsonists of their own happiness. What can sweet, sinless Jesus possibly know about the dark side of being human?

According to the scriptures, he knows more of the dark side than any of us. In fact, he knows more about pain, grief, loneliness, contradiction, shame, rejection, betrayal, anguish, depression, and guilt than all of us combined. For in the Garden of Gethsemane and on the hill of Calvary, Jesus took upon himself the sins and the pains of all the world. "Surely he hath borne our griefs, and carried our sorrows: yet we did esteem him stricken, smitten of God, and afflicted. But he was wounded for our transgressions, he was bruised for our iniquities: the chastisement of our peace was upon him; and with his stripes we are healed." (Isa. 53:4–5.)

I would like to draw attention to a few aspects of the Savior's vicarious suffering that often escape notice, but that are important for understanding our relationship with him. First, Jesus Christ did not just assume the *punishment* for our sins—he took the *guilt* as well. The sin, the experience itself with all of its negative consequences and ramifications, and not just the penalty for sin, became his. This is a crucial distinction. In the Atonement, Jesus does not just suffer our punishment for us, he becomes the guilty party in our place—*he becomes guilty for us and experiences our guilt:* "For he hath made him to be sin for us, who knew no sin; that we might be made the righteousness of God in him." (2 Cor. 5:21.)

In Christ there is a real transfer of guilt for innocence. Through the oneness of our covenant relationship, my guilt becomes Jesus' guilt, which he experienced and for which he suffered. At the same time, his innocence and perfection become mine, and I am rendered clean and worthy. In Christ our sins cease to be ours, and as far as the justice of God is concerned, we never committed them. Through the Atonement, we are not merely forgiven—we are rendered innocent once again.

If Jesus had assumed only the punishment for our sins but not the sins themselves, then when the penalty was paid, we would merely be "guilty but forgiven," instead of being sanctified through the Atonement, being perfect-in-

Christ, and being innocent and worthy of the kingdom of God and the presence of the Father. Part of the good news of Christ's atonement is that it renders us sinless, innocent, perfect, and celestial, which could not happen if we stubbornly insisted on suffering for our own sins. In that case, while our sins might eventually be paid for, they would remain *ours*, like canceled checks. Without the atonement of Christ that removes guilt as well as pays its penalty, we can never receive the innocence necessary to dwell in the presence of God. (Cf. D&C 1:31; 19:4–19.)

In experiencing both our punishment and our guilt, Jesus learned vicariously through the Atonement what it would have felt like to commit the sins he never committed. Thus, in a sense it would be correct to say that while Jesus committed no sins, he has been guilty of them all and knows intimately and personally their awful weight. Through us, by bearing our guilt, the sinless One experienced the full horror of human sinfulness, not merely the sins of one life, but of all lives—the sins of the world. Thus through his vicarious atonement, Jesus knows more than anyone about the dark side of being human. Even in that he is preeminent among us.

At one point in his vicarious agony, Jesus cried out, "My God, my God, why hast thou forsaken me?" (Matt. 27:46.) Is it possible that the Heavenly Father had really forsaken him? Could God have abandoned him in this most sacred and terrible hour? Yes, indeed. For Christ had become guilty of the sins of the world, guilty in our place. What happens to the rest of us when we are guilty of sin? The Spirit of

God withdraws from us, the heavens turn to brass, and we are left alone to stew in our guilt until we repent. In Gethsemane the best among us vicariously became the worst among us and suffered the very depths of hell. And as one who was guilty, the Savior experienced for the first time in his life the loss of the Spirit of God and of communion with his Father.

There was for him no support, no help—neither from his friends who slept through his agony, nor from the Spirit of God, which departed from him. No one has ever been as alone as Christ in the Garden. This is the significance of Isaiah 63:3: "I have trodden the winepress *alone*." (See also D&C 76:107.)

In Hebrew the word *Geth* [*gath*] means "press," and *semane* [*shemen*] means "oil" or "richness." *Gethsemane* therefore means "the press of oil" or the "press of richness." This refers to the huge presses for olives or grapes that were used to squeeze the oil or wine out of the pulp and that would be appropriately found in an olive grove like Gethsemane. Olives or grapes were put into the presses and squeezed until their juices flowed out of them.

What an appropriate name for the Garden where Jesus took upon himself the infinite weight of the sins and sorrows of the world and was pressed with that tremendous load until the blood flowed through his skin. (See Luke 22:44; D&C 19:18.) Just as olives and grapes are squeezed in the press, so Jesus, the true vine (see John 15:1), was squeezed in Gethsemane, "the press," until his richness, his juice, his oil, his blood, was shed for humanity. No wonder that the wine of the Last Supper and of the Christian sacrament is such a fitting symbol for the blood of Christ—they are obtained by the same process.

BELOW ALL THINGS

Still, however we may try to understand the Gethsemane experience, we are doomed to underestimate it. On one occasion when Joseph Smith complained to the Lord about his own trials and suffering, the Lord responded by saying, "The Son of Man hath descended below them all. Art thou greater than he?" (D&C 122:8.) Christ is described in several other places in scripture as having descended below all things: "He that ascended up on high, as also he descended below all things, in that he comprehended all things, that he might be in all and through all things, the light of truth." (D&C 88:6; see also Eph. 4:8–10.)

In Gethsemane and on Calvary, in his horrible suffering and death, the Savior descended below all things, just as in his resurrection he ascended above all things. Between those two events, Jesus Christ compassed either personally or vicariously the whole range of possible human experiences and circumstances from the worst to the best. He has been lower than the lowest of us and higher than the highest, so "that he comprehended all things." Both spatially as the light of creation and experientially as the Atoning One, Christ fills all things and is in and through all things. He has been everywhere.

Thus when we are tempted to think that our sins have put us beyond the understanding or reach of God, we are simply mistaken, and we grossly underestimate the scope of the Atonement. However low we may fall, our Redeemer has already been there, and he went there for the sole purpose of finding and bringing us lost sheep back. I have occasionally heard people say things like, "How can I come back to Church, or pray, or approach God after what I've done. I've sunk too low; I've put myself beyond his reach. I'm too vile to save." To this the Savior responds essentially, "I know where you are; I've *been* where you are — and worse than that. I know what you're feeling, for I have felt it. I remember my own pain when I went through it, and my heart aches for you. But I want you back. I'll even carry you back, if you'll let me." No matter how lost we get, Jesus Christ, the way back, the door home, is always at our elbow.

AN INFINITE ATONEMENT

The suffering of Jesus Christ in the Garden and on the cross exceeded the combined suffering of all human beings. The suffering of Jesus was not just tough pain and a bad death, it was not just the most painful of all human experiences and deaths. The suffering of Christ was cumulative; it was in fact infinite. When Christ descended below all things, he crossed the line from the finite, that which can be measured, to the infinite. And as his suffering was infinite, so now is his glory infinite, and infinite also is his power to save. "Wherefore, it must needs be an infinite atonement — save it should be an infinite atonement this corruption could not put on incorruption." (2 Ne. 9:7.) "Therefore there can be nothing which is short of an infinite

atonement which will suffice for the sins of the world."
(Alma 34:12; see also 2 Ne. 25:16; Alma 34:10, 14; D&C
19:10–19.)

Human nature makes us want to quantify, to measure
the atonement of Christ, but his ordeal is off any scale; it
is beyond our comprehension. Jesus bore not just the sins
of the world, but the sorrows, pains, and sicknesses of the
world as well: "He shall go forth, suffering pains and afflic-
tions and temptations of every kind, and this that the word
might be fulfilled which saith he will take upon him the
pains and the sicknesses of his people. And he will take
upon him death, that he may loose the bands of death which
bind his people; and he will take upon him their infirmities,
that his bowels may be filled with mercy, according to the
flesh, that he may know according to the flesh how to succor
his people according to their infirmities." (Alma 7:11–12.)

How many people have suffered how much pain in our
world just for today? How many people in how many hos-
pitals right now all over the world are crying out for another
shot to ease the pain? Just today? Yet the suffering of Jesus
Christ in the Garden and on the cross exceeded the combined suffering of all human beings from our first parents
to the Last Day, for this world and for all worlds created by
his power.

All the negative aspects of human existence brought
about by the Fall, Jesus Christ absorbed into himself. He
experienced vicariously in Gethsemane all the private griefs
and heartaches, all the physical pains and handicaps, all the
emotional burdens and depressions of the human family.

He knows the loneliness of those who don't fit in or who aren't handsome or pretty. He knows what it's like to choose up teams and be the last one chosen. He knows the anguish of parents whose children go wrong. He knows the private hell of the abused child or spouse. He knows all these things personally and intimately because he lived them in the Gethsemane experience. Having personally lived a perfect life, he then chose to experience our imperfect lives. In that infinite Gethsemane experience, the meridian of time, the center of eternity, he lived a billion billion lifetimes of sin, pain, disease, and sorrow.

God uses no magic wand to simply wave bad things into nonexistence. The sins that he remits, he remits by making them his own and suffering them. The pain and heartaches that he relieves, he relieves by suffering them himself. These things can be shared and absorbed, but they cannot be simply wished or waved away. They must be suffered. Thus we owe him not only for our spiritual cleansing from sin, but for our physical, mental, and emotional healings as well, for he has borne these infirmities for us also. All that the Fall put wrong, the Savior in his atonement puts right. It is all part of his infinite sacrifice — of his infinite gift.

For this reason, to be able to bear an infinite weight of agony, Jesus needed to have an infinite, divine Father. From Mary he inherited the ability to die, but from his Father he inherited the ability to live if he so chose. Therefore his life could not be taken without his consent — he had power over death. (See John 10:17–18.) If you or I had gone into the press of Gethsemane and shouldered that load of sin and pain, it would have squashed us like bugs, snuffed us out instantly. But because he was the Son of God and had power over death, his life could not be taken until he laid it down of his own will.

In the Garden and on the cross he said, in essence, "I will suffer this agony; I will sustain it; I will endure this for their sakes and hold on to it until they are saved." As Elder Neal A. Maxwell has said, "The cumulative weight of all mortal sins — past, present, and future — pressed upon that perfect, sinless, and sensitive Soul! All our infirmities and sicknesses were somehow, too, a part of the awful arithmetic of the Atonement. . . . His suffering — as it were, *enormity* multiplied by *infinity* — evoked His later soul-cry on the cross, and it was a cry of forsakenness."[3]

Did his infinite agony tempt him to lay down his life and end his suffering *before* the price was fully paid? Was his greatest temptation to abandon his weaker brothers and sisters and seek relief from an infinity of pain by dying prematurely? Perhaps. All he had to do was let go, and the pain would stop, but you and I would be lost. And so second by second, hour by hour, he embraced his agony; he could not rest, but he would not die, not until it was finished, not until we were saved with him. Thus, when the Victor comes to earth again clothed in power and glory, the angels will declare his infinite and eternal victory: "It is finished; it is finished! The Lamb of God hath overcome and trodden the

---

[3]Neal A. Maxwell, "Willing to Submit," *Ensign*, May 1985, p. 73.

wine-press alone, even the wine-press of the fierceness of the wrath of Almighty God." (D&C 88:106.)

The divine victim has answered the demands of justice in the Garden of the Press and on Calvary, and he did it alone, and he did it for you and me. This gives him the right to claim those who enter into his covenant, to bring each one of us under his wing and say, "I've paid for this one; this one is mine"—"Father, behold the sufferings and death of him who did no sin, in whom thou wast well pleased; behold the blood of thy Son which was shed, the blood of him whom thou gavest that thyself might be glorified; wherefore, Father, spare these my brethren that believe on my name, that they may come unto me and have everlasting life." (D&C 45:4–5.)

And that is the best news of all.

INDEX

Adam, need of Savior for, 55
"After all we can do," discussion
of, 90–92
Analogy: parent-child
relationship, 4–5, 62–63;
electricity, 12; lifeguard, 18;
bank account, 24; marriage
covenant, 24–25; corporation,
28–29; athletics, 29–30; race,
30; bicycle, 30–32; yoke, 44;
Hawaii trip, 68–69; talents,
70, 95; dream of horse and
cliff, 79–80; Church welfare
program, 88–89; weight room,
101–2; swimming lesson,
106–7. *See also* Parable
Athletics, analogy of, 29–30
Atonement: definition of, 7–8;
joins us with Christ, 8; why,
is difficult to accept, 9–12;
reconciles imperfect people to
God, 13–14, 111–12; receiving
righteousness through, 20–21;
perfection obtained through,
23–24, 27; and the covenant

relationship, 33–34; lifts curse
of the law, 44; all can be
justified in Christ through,
48–51; answers justice and
mercy, 57–59; is the grace of
Christ, 61, 65–66; must be
acknowledged, 69; as the gift,
82–83; Jesus suffered our
punishment and guilt in, 117;
infinite, 121–25. *See also*
Jesus Christ
Attitude, 51–55. *See also* Efforts

Balance of good and evil, 1–2
Bank account, analogy of, 24
Beliefs, traditional Christian, 11,
18, 48
Bicycle, parable of, 30–32
Burdens, 44

Calvary, Jesus suffering at, 116–
20
Carnal nature. *See* Sin
Child-and-parent relationship,
analogies of, 4–5, 62–63

127

Christian beliefs, traditional, 11, 18, 48
Church, demands of, 100–102
Cliff, analogy of, 79–80
Commandments: in law of Moses, 38–39; keeping, 42, 45–48. *See also* Efforts
Corporation, analogy of, 28–29
Covenant relationship: we form, with Christ, 24–26; likened to race, 30; bicycle parable is example of, 30–33; definition of, 35–36; Old Testament examples of, 36; new and everlasting, 36–37; of faith, 43; requirements within, 45; terms of, 47–48; universal yet individualized participation in, 49; renewal of, 52–54; misunderstanding of, 58; as covenant of grace, 66; is sufficient for salvation, 69, 104–5; obligations of partners in, 71–72, 90, 97; God discerns honest hearts in, 86; breaking, 86–87; requires best efforts, 87–88; how to know, is accepted, 94; transfers our guilt for Jesus' innocence, 117

Defaults in life, 60
Despair. *See* Hopelessness
Dilemma: great, 1–5; answer to great, 7–8; between keeping and trying to keep commandments, 45–47
Docetism, 114
Dream of horse and cliff, 79–80

Efforts: individual, can make you just, 27–28; as related to perfection, 27–28, 98; put

forth best, 87–88; how to know, are acceptable, 92–95; vary, 95–97; best, accepted by Church, 100–103
Electricity, analogy of, 12
Endurance to end, 49, 106
Example: doubters, 10–11; brother of Jared, 18–20; Janet Robinson, 14–17; Nephi, 21–23; "perfect" missionary, 74–75; proud man, 80–82; tough woman, 95–97; Mother Theresa, 99; divorced mother, 100

Fairness. *See* Justice, law of
Faith: in Christ, 9, 12; lacking, in Christ, 10–12, 107; of brother of Jared, 18–20; of Nephi, 21–23; versus works argument, 69–72; demonstrating, 88–89
Father-and-son relationship, analogy of, 4–5
Fear, 23, 107

Gethsemane, Garden of: experience of Jesus in, 116, 121–25; meaning of, 119; Jesus descended below all things in, 120–21
God: does not tolerate sin, 1–3; infinite love of, 7–8; love of, precedes grace, 63–65; spirit of, 118–19. *See also* Jesus Christ
Grace: definition of, 61; parent-child analogy to, 62–63; examples of, 63–64, 91; as conditional on human behavior, 64; in Book of Mormon, 67–68; is not automatic, 68; resisting, 72–